cinematic motion

film directing

cinematic motion

a workshop for staging scenes

by
steven d. katz

Published by Michael Wiese Productions,
11288 Ventura Boulevard,
Suite #821,
Studio City, CA 91604
(818) 379-8799, (818) 986-3408 (FAX).

Cover design by Charles Field
Cover photograph by Charles Field
Additional photography by Geraldine Overton
Interior design and layout by Steven D. Katz and Catherine
Bandoian
Illustrations by Steven D. Katz
Composition by Brad Walrod/High Text Graphics

Printed by Braun-Brumfield, Ann Arbor, Michigan
Manufactured in the United States of America

Copyright 1992 by Michael Wiese Productions
First printing, November 1992

All rights reserved. No part of this book may be reproduced in
any form or by any means without the permission in writing
from the author, except for the inclusion of brief quotations in
a review.

Library of Congress Cataloging-in-Publication Data
Katz, Steven D. (Steven Douglas),
    Film directing—cinematic motion: a workshop for staging
scenes/by Steven D. Katz
        p.   cm.
    ISBN 0–941188–14–0
    1. Blocking (Motion pictures)   2. Motion pictures—
Production and direction.   I. Title   II. Title: Cinematic
motion.
PN1995.9.P7K37   1992   92–35112
791.43′0233—dc20   CIP

ACKNOWLEDGEMENTS

Several of the most knowledgeable filmmakers in the movie business shared their ideas and insights with me during the writing of *Cinematic Motion*. They are featured individually in several chapters, but the interviews could only include a small portion of their hard-earned experience. Thank you, John Sayles, Harold Michelson, Ralph S. Singleton, Dusty Smith, Allen Daviau, ASC and Emily Laskin of the American Film Institute.

Many thanks to my friends at Virtus Corporation for creating Virtus WalkThrough, a magical visualization tool that allowed me to create illustrations that would otherwise have been impossible. I am particularly indebted to Alan Scott at Virtus for his technical support.

Finally, I would also like to thank cinematographer Kevin Lombard for his thoughts on camera movement and equipment and other photographic aspects of staging.

TABLE OF CONTENTS

INTRODUCTION

Cinematic Motion started out as a reference manual for filmmakers. It was described to the publisher as "A collection of blocking strategies covering a wide range of dramatic situations and camera styles, an easily-accessed resource for directors at every level."

This would be fun to write, I thought, with lots of opportunities for dreaming up camera moves and complex sequence shots. Naturally, I wouldn't have to worry about overtime or meal penalties because in the storyboard panels of my imaginary movie, the budget was unlimited. On this best of all possible sets, the sun would shine through perfect clouds, the crew would never grumble about lunch and magic hour, when needed, would last for as long as there was film.

But before many pages were typed, I realized something was missing from the staging examples. They were too easy to create. Perhaps I should add a few practical words about equipment failure or some comments about the long hours required for rigging lights and, Oh, let's not forget about shooting in 105 degree heat....

As reality crept into the designing of the staging diagrams, my role became that of a production manager. Like the muse in reverse, I found myself pointing out the potential difficulties of each staging strategy and asking whether all that coverage was really necessary. At last, I began to appreciate the production manager's unenviable task of giving the director all he wants—at a price the producer can afford.

This is how the reference manual on staging became a survival guide for filmmakers. In its final form, the primary focus of the book remains the staging ideas chosen for their artistic merit, but now there are practical evaluations of the staging examples so that directors can better develop a sense of what is the right solution for any given situation.

Hopefully, this is a fairer book. Fairer because, by including the cost in time and artistic energy attached to any staging approach, a filmmaker will not place impossible demands on himself or his collaborators. In the movies, it is important that your artistic aims be true as well as high.

None of this would matter if the staging examples in this book were formula solutions for simple coverage. They're not. This book is for risk-takers. Some of the staging examples are technically simple, others require substantial choreography. But the underlying assumption is that the filmmaker wants to explore the dramatic potential of the camera to the fullest.

Every day on the set a director asks himself, "How can I best stage this scene?" And every day the production manager asks the director, "Can you get all this shot by the end of the day?" The success of any movie is greatly dependent on how these questions are resolved and ultimately it is up to the director to find the right answers. Knowing how to get all your camera setups within the day's shooting schedule comes from experience, experience which ultimately affects a director's creative success.

HOW TO USE THIS BOOK

Even though storyboards have been the accepted way of illustrating shot-flow design in the movies for nearly sixty years, there is no standard system of notation. Each production illustrator develops his own way of representing the complex moving action in a shot using arrows, panels within panels, multiple positions of moving figures, written description and any other technique that makes a sequence clear.

Oftentimes, 4 or 5 separate panels are required to describe just a few seconds of action and there is always the danger that the overall feeling of a scene is lost when too much description is used. Even so, the prime purpose of a storyboard is to convey specific and technically-accurate descriptions of cinematic technique. While every storyboard artist hopes that his work "reads" well, it is often necessary to look over the panels more than once to understand the choreography, which brings us to the notational method used in this book.

For the sake of clarity, every storyboard in this book is accompanied by a diagram of the scene space. The storyboards show what the audience will see on the screen, while the diagrams show the camera path and choreography required to stage the action taking place in the storyboards. Some of the choreography is complex so you will probably have to look through a storyboard more than once to understand how the scenes were staged.

To help you better understand the illustrations, I've included a description of how the storyboards and the various symbols are used throughout the book. If you spend some time familiarizing yourself with the techniques shown below, you will find it much easier to use the book.

STORYBOARDS

The storyboards used in this book are drawn in the 1:1.85 wide screen aspect ratio which is the typical release format for most American films.

The page layout for the staging illustrations is a two-page spread with top and bottom pairs of storyboard/diagram illustrations.

Storyboards appear on left hand pages and are numbered.

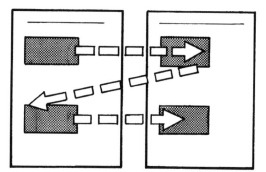

Diagrams accompanying the storyboards appear on right hand pages.

Description of each shot is printed directly underneath the storyboard panel. When dialogue is used, it appears underneath the description, as shown below.

Description appears here.

ANN: Dialogue appears here.

All storyboards are numbered and the accompanying set diagram will have the same number following the letter D. The number for storyboards and diagrams refers to the shot. Sometimes several storyboards are required to

explain sequential stages of a dolly shot and in this case the shot number won't change. Instead, the various panels are distinguished alphabetically.

For instance, the first of four panels showing an uninterrupted crane shot would be numbered. In this example shot 1 is the crane move and storyboard panels 1a through 1c show different stages in the shot. Ellipsis ... is included in the description as an added reminder that the shot is continuing as shown below:

1

1

1a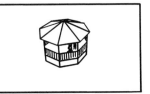

1a Consecutive letters after a number...

1b

1b... indicate that the shot...

1c

1c... is continuing.

2 A change in number indicates a shot change.

To make a shot change clear, Cut To: appears at the beginning of the new shot description.

ARROWS OUTSIDE THE FRAME

Arrows appearing on the right side of the storyboard frame indicate the movement of the camera. The arrows are drawn in perspective to show if the camera is dollying in or out, dollying left or right.

If the camera movement is a lateral pan, the arrow will not be drawn in perspective. Examples are shown below.

  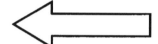 

DOLLY IN	DOLLY OUT	PAN	DOLLY AROUND	CRANE

ARROWS INSIDE THE FRAME

An outline arrow indicates the movement of a subject.

If a subject enters the frame from off-screen, the arrow will pass through the border of the frame.

Similarly, if a subject exits the frame, the arrow will pass beyond the border of the frame.

An arrow path that begins at a subject, indicates the path that the subject takes.

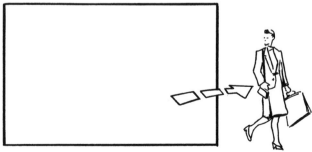

SET DIAGRAMS

A perspective overview of the set or scene space will be included to help clarify the choreography. These diagrams are based on computer models created in Virtus WalkThrough, a computer program that is rapidly becoming a director's best visualization tool.

In most cases, these diagrams will show the entire set or location from the perspective of a person standing behind the camera. If a moving shot is being illustrated, the set diagrams will include the path of the camera.

D1

There are two types of camera symbols. The first shows the outline of the camera. This indicates the beginning of a camera move. The second type of camera symbol is solid black. This indicates the final position of a move.

In a few cases, when the camera movement is complex, intermediate stages of camera movement are shown. This will be indicated by multiple outline cameras.

A pan move is indicated by a camera symbol with a curved arrow through the middle.

**CAMERA
STARTS HERE**

**CAMERA
STOPS HERE**

PAN

The path of moving actors is shown by broken lines connecting outline and solid figure symbols. As with the moving camera, outline symbols indicate the starting point of an actor's move while a solid black symbol indicates the final position for an actor.

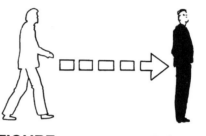

**FIGURE
STARTS HERE**　　　**FIGURE
STOPS HERE**

SCHEMATIC
DIAGRAMS

Accompanying some of the storyboards are aerial views of the set or location. The general rule for symbols already established will also apply to the set diagrams. This means that outline symbols (for camera and actors) indicate the beginning of a move while solid black symbols indicate the end of a move.

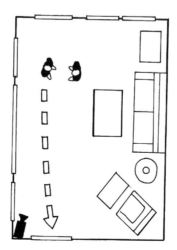

CONSISTENCY   In the majority of illustrations the format and symbols shown here will be followed, however, there are exceptions. In these special cases, notes will appear alongside illustrations. For example, there were times when a solid black camera would have been difficult to see in front of a dark background and in those instances the outline of the camera was used instead.

My aim in *Cinematic Motion* was to write a book accessible to both new and seasoned directors. Therefore, the stagings presented in the following chapters are explained with the expectation that the fundamentals of editing, photography, cinematic technique and motion picture production are familiar to the reader. This includes a knowledge of shot types, the use of the shot, reverse shot pattern, the line of action and other stylistic conventions of the continuity style.

Chapters 1, and 3, however, offer an overview of staging theory which is not absolutely necessary to understand the staging examples if you are already familiar with basic camera movement.

The ideas presented here tend to emphasize camera choreography and the master shot rather than cutting as a way of varying the viewing angle and directing the viewer's attention. You will, however, find both approaches covered in the book, since in actual practice, they are complementary techniques.

If you are interested in the staging possibilities of the static frame, the subject has been covered in many books on film including my own, *Shot by Shot,* which, in an informal way, lays the groundwork for the stagings in *Cinematic Motion.*

part 1
staging: the process

1 STAGING: THE DIRECTOR

Staging is at the center of the director's craft. It is the point of contact for acting, cinematography and editing, the three areas for which a director is expected to provide the finished design.

No one on the set, from the cinematographer to the prop master, can begin work until the director makes two decisions—first, where the camera will be placed and second, how the actors will move in front of the camera.

Any director who looks beyond just getting two or three pages of script in the can per day, that is, a director with a vision, will at some moment stand on the set or location with a case of butterflies thinking about the staging possibilities. Every director knows (or soon learns) that staging is not a series of individual decisions, but is really a plan that determines the work of the entire production team on any day of principal photography.

Some directors discover the plan on the set without much preparation. Others, with the gift for previsualizing entire sequences, can organize their ideas into detailed shot lists or storyboards. But no matter what method a director uses, his ability to work with the camera and the actors will improve with experience. Experience on the set, however, is hard to come by if you are starting out, and even working directors spend more time waiting for the next project than on the set practicing their craft.

One way that directors can sharpen their staging skills when they are not at work, is to simplify the seemingly endless considerations that go into staging on a set by conceptualizing them as patterns of movement, and as a vocabulary of techniques. That, simply put, is the method we will be using here.

Basically, a director is dealing with three factors when he composes a scene for the camera:

Narrative considerations

Dramatic considerations

Pictorial considerations

Narrative considerations are the specific actions described in the script. For example, a man drives into a self-service gas station and exits his car to pump gas. In this case, the action is straightforward and there is little room for staging interpretation. But if the scene takes place at a party and the characters are free to move through the rooms of a house, the director and the actors are free to move anywhere.

Dramatic considerations include the elements which color our emotional understanding of a scene. They fall into two categories: point of view and dramatic emphasis.

POINT OF VIEW

The manipulation of point of view in a scene is the single most significant decision in determining camera placement. While a single, consistent narrative voice is typical of a short story or a novel, a fluid point of view is common in narrative film. Point of view can change rapidly from one character to another in a scene, favoring one or the other, or it can maintain a neutral stance.

A director controls point of view by manipulating narrative logic, eye-contact and shot-size. Narrative logic means that we learn about the story by following the actions of one or more characters. If a scene opens in a liquor store and follows a clerk for several moments before two teenagers enter, we are being encouraged to see the scene from the shopkeeper's point of view. Conversely, if we follow the teenagers outside the store before being introduced to the clerk, when the teenagers go inside, we will tend to identify with the teenagers.

Eye-contact is a more subtle cue in the control of point of view, but is still a very potent factor. For example, when an actor is looking toward the camera, we are placed in a closer relationship with that subject. Even if the actor has his back to us and the camera frames the actor's field of vision, we are being asked to share his point of view. Framing this same action so that we see the actor in profile has the opposite effect, placing us in a more neutral relationship with the subject.

Shot-size is another way in which a director can guide our identification with a character. Generally speaking, the tighter the shot, the greater our sense of intimacy with a subject. This enhances our sense of identification.

DRAMATIC EMPHASIS

Dramatic emphasis is related to shot size. It can heighten or diminish an actor's performance, physical action, and dramatic events. Any actor can be made to control our attention merely by how he is placed in the frame.

Lighting, art direction, the choice of lens and editing all help control dramatic emphasis, but in terms of staging, our primary concern is shot size and the placement of subjects in the frame. Contrast is a major factor. For instance, moving from a medium shot to a closeup of a subject is normally perceived as a way of emphasizing the importance of a subject. But it is also possible (though less common) to achieve emphasis by moving from a closeup of a subject to a wide shot.

The last staging category includes the pictorial considerations. These are the graphic elements such as composition, framing, lighting and the photographic properties of the lens. The pictorial qualities of a shot are the easiest to visualize because they are less dependent on other shots in a sequence for their full effect.

When a director looks through the viewfinder of the camera, he sees all the pictorial qualities that will appear on the screen. He doesn't have to imagine how they will change when edited into a sequence of shots. In this sense, pictorial considerations are less cinematic than dramatic emphasis and point of view. A director will take all three factors into consideration (narrative considerations, dramatic emphasis and pictorial considerations) when staging a scene. The way in which a director chooses to emphasize these factors defines his staging method.

THE DRAMATIC CIRCLE OF ACTION

In staging there are essentially two approaches to space. One is to place the camera in the action; the second is to place it outside the action. Since action can include anything from an angry mob to an intimate conversation between a couple in bed, a director has to define what part of the action he will include in the frame. The space in which the action takes place is called the dramatic circle of action.

A camera can be placed in the circle of action or outside the circle of action, and an edited sequence can combine shots photographed from either placement. A moving camera can go inside the circle of action and out again or vice versa. It is also possible to move the dramatic circle of action since the subjects of a shot are frequently mobile.

MASTER AND SEQUENCE SHOTS

A director can stage a scene for a single camera setup or cut together shots of the scene taken from different angles. In a single camera setup, a director can choreograph his actors so that different views of them are seen, even though there is no editing. Camera movement can be added so that several views of the scene are included in one uninterrupted shot. A highly choreographed shot that covers lots of action is usually referred to as a sequence shot, though it is really a version of a master shot. Regardless of how it is labeled, the distinguishing factor is that a single shot is employed to cover most of the action in the script for a given scene.

MULTIPLE SETUPS AND COVERAGE

Using multiple setups in a scene is an editorial style of reporting action. The multiple-setup style achieves dramatic emphasis through a change in viewpoint. Coverage grows out of the director's need to try different ways of shooting a scene even though it is inevitable that much of what is shot will be discarded.

Because editing means taking an action and breaking it into shorter segments of time, it may seem that camera movement and complex choreography are not as necessary as they would be in a long, uninterrupted shot of the same action. While it is true that both styles are capable of achieving the same results—multiple viewpoints—they are by no means mutually exclusive. There are many instances when complex staging is combined with fast cutting, merging the sequence shot style and the multiple-setup style of staging.

Related to the stylistic approaches of the sequence shot and multiple camera setups is the director's approach to the scene space. Some directors stage action for the camera, while others stage action and photograph it. This recalls the classic opposition of realism and expressionism in film theory. Realism argues for the integrity of the scene space and linear time, and advocates documentary techniques with little intrusion of editorial commentary. Conversely, expressionism advocates the dramatic use of the camera and cinematic technique to illuminate the truth. In recent years there has been a healthy reconciliation between these views since neither approach offers a truly objective view.

There is no question, however, that realism and expressionism are different styles of filmmaking that relate to how a director views the action in front of the camera. In narrative film, it is the difference between rehearsing a scene in strict accordance with the actor's choices and the events in the script—and the direction of actors to achieve dramatic effects through the use of the camera. As with any generalization there are numerous exceptions and contradictions. Still, directors do tend toward one approach or the other.

In practice, a director who is closer to the realist style will most likely allow the actors considerable freedom to move in the scene. This is usually best accommodated by a hand-held camera, Steadicam or a light camera on a tripod.

A director who is closer to the expressionistic style will carefully plan his shots and take a great deal of time to control every aspect of the frame. Actors will be required to precisely hit certain marks and to keep to exact timings of specific actions. Often it is necessary to position the actors in ways that look unreal on the set, but which will seem natural on film.

Of course, no director is tied to any one approach and can call upon either style to achieve his interpretation of a scene. In fact, all the factors discussed in this chapter are highly flexible. When a director begins to visualize a script, the imagination takes over, and a series of shots begin to emerge. It is not until a production begins that a director is required to consider the practicality of any given staging approach. This is when a director learns to be flexible, to call upon his craft and resourcefulness. At this time, the production manager and line producer become the director's most important support team. Because all staging styles require different amounts of time to shoot, a well-prepared director should have more than a passing familiarity with the process of scheduling a movie.

INTERVIEW JOHN SAYLES

John Sayles is a highly regarded novelist and short story writer. He financed his first feature film, *Return of the Secaucus Seven,* by writing screenplays. Since then he has written, directed, edited (and occasionally acted) in six independent feature films including, *Lianna, Baby It's You, The Brother From Another Planet, Matewan, Eight Men Out and City of Hope.*

You have a reputation for doing a great deal of previsualization. Why?

Part of it is because I am a writer and part of it is really just economics. Eight Men Out *is a good example. I had story-boarded all the baseball scenes in* Eight Men Out *several years earlier and when we finally made the film, Bob Richardson, the cinematographer, and I went out to the field where we were shooting. The one thing about storyboarding baseball, is that it is always 90 feet between base and home. All the geography is very predictable. You know that if you have the camera at first base shooting towards third, the pitcher is always going to be in the shot. So we went to each of our storyboard positions and tested lenses to see how much of the background would be in the shot. We had a production assistant in the stands walking in a vector to locate the outer edges of our frame. Then we'd mark that and then go look at the map of the ball-park to see how many extras we'd need to fill the fans in the background. So I*

knew that if we had 200 extras, we could use the 50mm lens, but if there were only 100 extras, I would have to use the 75mm lens. If there were less than 100 people, I would have to use the 100mm lens and in that case maybe it would be better to shoot that scene another day.

What other techniques or equipment do you use to previsualize the staging of a scene?

In the case of the long Steadicam shots in City of Hope *we went out to the actual locations in preproduction and worked out the shots substituting production assistants for the actors. They walked through the scene talking and reading the script. We followed them with a Steadicam operator and a video assistant.*

Do you ever wait until you are on the set to work out the blocking?

I generally only do that if it's a very emotional scene. In that situation what I don't want to do is let the actors worry about hitting a tape mark and things like that. For example, in the big argument/fight scene between Vincent Spano and Roseanne Arquette in Baby It's You, *Michael Bauhas, the cinematographer, and I just watched them at three quarter emotion two or three times. We whispered ideas to each other as the actors worked. We ended up covering it pretty simply, but what was clear during the run through was that the actors figured out where they were generally going to be fairly quickly. So we gave it a slightly looser lighting plan and a looser camera and we didn't lock the camera down ever.*

By giving the actors more breathing room do you have less control over the purely visual elements?

Yes. The lighting is always a compromise and a little less specific than when we know where the actors are going to move.

If this loose way of blocking a scene is an exception what is your usual approach to staging?

Because we have to work on a short schedule, I have to pretty much block the scenes even before the actors get there. What I do for them is to try to make the blocking have a reason behind it. So in

City of Hope, *instead of giving very specific marks, what I would try to do is say, 'OK, you're going to walk along the sidewalk until you get to the cars and then you're going to walk between them and go across the street.' And then I only leave one gap between the cars so the actors have only one logical place to go.*

Describe a typical day as you prepare to stage a scene.

Generally, what I do first thing in the morning is I talk to the cameraman about how we are going to cover the first scene. Then I go in with the actors and get hair and makeup done and talk to them about two things—one is what the morning looks like in terms of the schedule. I usually only talk about the morning and the afternoon schedule because I don't want them to carry too much information—you only want people to have the next three or four shots in their head. This is so the actors will have a general idea of what we are going to shoot that day. I'll tell them what kind of coverage we are going to get because I want them to be able to pace themselves emotionally.

This is especially helpful if they know they are going to be off-screen for the first half of a scene. Because I've been an actor, one of the things I've learned is that you can do pretty much anything you want off-screen. This can be very useful because if you do your off-screen stuff first, then you can be trying things out that you use later when the camera turns and you're the subject of the shot.

[Note: Off-screen in this case means a camera setup like a closeup, medium shot or any other single in which one actor is on camera speaking with another actor who is participating in the scene but is not in the shot.]

The other thing I do with the actors in the morning is I'll go over, emotionally and sequentially, where they are in the story. Because you shoot movies out of sequence, I let the actor know what scenes preceded the one he is about to do and give him an overall sense of time and place.

How does letting an actor know what the coverage is going to be, help him with his performance?

You don't want an actor to spend himself emotionally in coverage that does not emphasize him.

For example, a master shot as opposed to a closeup. When there is a master shot that is just going to establish the opening of a scene, very often I'll say, 'OK, I'm only going to use this shot to get us into the room. Consider the rest of the take a rehearsal. Give your performance a shot, but don't blow yourself out.' And then the actor has an idea of how to pace himself for that scene and he'll know when the real money shot is coming. It's very helpful to know that because once an actor has peaked, it's very hard to get that intensity back.

What other useful things can you tell the actor about the staging?

In a master shot, it's helpful to know that you don't have to worry about your props. You can wave your cocktail glass around, you can scratch your head with your hand, rock in the seat and all that type of stuff. On the other hand, if there's going to be a lot of coverage which is more likely to show up any discontinuity, then as a film actor, you want to know that. In that case, an actor would want to simplify his business so he doesn't have to worry about keeping track of a lot of gestures or movement. Sometimes I suggest that an actor go over to the script supervisor and say, 'Keep track of what I'm doing in rehearsal and tell me if I'm really inconsistent.' And the actor can get himself *more consistent so that he doesn't have to do four more takes because he used the wrong hand in his hair in the OTS shot.*

How do you deal with actors who reach their performance peak at very different times?

You find out pretty quickly how they work and what makes them better or worse. Whether they're good at long pieces, or if you should cut their scenes up, or whether they are good at continuity or not. You basically try to handicap the scene for those actors.

For instance, with kids I'll start out very conservatively planning to do a lot of coverage so I can piece the performance together if I have to. But if the kid turns out to be someone who can carry a scene, I'll shoot less coverage and I'll let him carry the ball a bit more and let him create his own moment instead of my cutting one together. If it's two actors who have very different warm-up speeds, I'll use the technical rehearsal for the actor who needs more warm up. I'll read lines with him until he is closer to being up to speed and then bring the other actor in. Especially if it's a two-shot. If it's opposing coverage for close-ups, then I'll shoot the actor who warms

up quickly first. I'll use the actor who is slower off-camera. And I'll even direct them off-camera and have them try different things.

Do the actors like or prefer the types of very long master shots you used in *City of Hope* because it is more like theater?

I think they do if they feel in control of it. But an uninterrupted shot may be very unlike theater. In City of Hope, *some of the actors entered in the middle of the scene and really had to hit precise marks and timings. Sometimes they had to come in out of the blue and they didn't always have a chance to get themselves up to speed. They had a lot to think about besides their craft. For instance, there's a scene in* City of Hope *when the characters of Connie and Jo Anne, the neighborhood ladies, are in the Mayor's office. They showed up in the middle of the shot and they're at the bottom of the stairs with the actor Joe Garfazzi who's playing the Mayor's assistant. They appeared three minutes into the scene and had to wait to hear a certain line which was their cue. They had to time their entrance and the volume of what they were doing so that they hit the camera at exactly the right*

■

point. They had to worry about a number of technical things and that was very, very hard for them.

So the pressure is on not to blow the take which includes the 2 or 3 minutes that came before?

The further down in the shot you appear, the more pressure there is. What you try to do is give the actors the feeling 'Hey, look, we're going to do this a bunch of times. Try to keep three of these with no technical problems so you'll get a couple of shots at this.' And that takes some of the pressure off. Certainly there's more pressure with a low-budget movie like ours.

Most of the very long masters in City of Hope were shot with the Steadicam. Tell me about explaining the shots to the actors.

The way we would proceed with that is, I'd explain the general blocking. For instance, I'd say to the actors, 'I want you to start at this point and stop over here and then climb these stairs.' And we would just start following it with the Steadicam. But, as I mentioned before, we had worked a lot of this out in pre-production using production assistants. So, technically, the Stedicam operator

and the crew knew what was going to happen and the actors could concentrate on dialogue. The Steadicam has video assist built in so we could adjust things easily. Sometimes it's a matter of saying 'Well, what if we had a body cross here, would it hide the lights?'

What are the technical problems you run into in covering so much territory in one shot?

When you are doing those 360 degree shots in an interior, you have a real problem hiding the lights. And sometimes you have to use a body to mask a light. Or sometimes you have to have an extra hold the light, and as soon as the camera gets near him, he has to duck behind something. Then, as soon as the camera passes, the extra reappears with the light because it's needed again. In one of the bar scenes in City of Hope, *the character I played is in the scene. I had a Sony Watchman [for video assist] so I could see how the shot was going just up to the point when I was about to come on screen. Then, I would do my part, and once the camera went past me and I saw the back of the cameraman, I would take the Watchman from behind the bar again and watch the rest of the scene.*

Do you have time and the budget for rehearsals?

The only time I've had time for that is on Eight Men Out *and* Baby It's You. *On* Baby It's You, *I got three days when I got all the girls together who were supposed to be high school friends. We just hung out and didn't talk about the movie or the script. We talked about boys and cars and records and this was to get the girls used to each other and give their relationship some sense of rhythm and camaraderie. On* Eight Men Out, *we had a training camp for a week, but we didn't work on any of the dialogue. We were there to work specifically on physical workouts for the baseball.*

Without rehearsals how do you help the actors prepare for the role?

For a film, I'd send each of the actors a one or two page bio of the character. I prefer to talk to the actor about the situation and character on the day we shoot and I often end up using the first take. If you can do enough cold rehearsals so that the technical side is down, you get an immediacy with the first take. And I'll just tell the actor to play the moment. This is often better than when they play all the preparation.

Sometimes, especially a theater-trained actor, will add so many levels of meaning to a simple scene, that it gets in the way of the moment. So sometimes the first two or three takes is to get rid of too much preparation. Other times it really does feel like the action is a little shallow. That's when I will stop and talk about the character a little.

As a director, you try not to get the actors to play more than two things at the same time. You might tell them that they are angry, but are trying to hold it back. Or you tell them they are happy, but a little nervous. That is something that will read. But when you tell the actor 'OK, you're happy, but you're nervous and you are secretly worried about whether you've left the stove on,' what this tends to do is make the pause between lines interminable and the audience doesn't get anything.

How much time do you permit yourself to get a long master shot when it is being substituted for coverage?

In City of Hope, *there's the shot in the Mayor's office which is a five-to-seven minute Steadicam shot. We'll give that a morning. We'll have been there already and have done a rehearsal without actors and we'll know what hallways we're going to be in. This way the director of photography knows where he is going to put his lights and he knows where the bodies are going to move.*

Then it's a matter of working with the actors and the camera operator. In the case of a Steadicam operator, you have to deal with getting all your cables straight and not tripping over the sound-man. If there's a move that's just too hard or awkward or doesn't look good, you find ways to re-block slightly and then you put in your extras and do camera wipes [extras crossing the frame to give a sense of a real, inhabited loca-tion]. I'll give a five-to-seven minute shot like that a morning. You can give it three days, but with the budgets I work with I don't have three days.

How many takes did it take you to get the long Steadicam shot in *City of Hope*?

I think we ended up doing ten takes and only about four of those actually went to the end. And in between the aborted takes, you might work some things out with the Steadicam operator or you might work out something with the actors, but that's really only two hours of shooting.

Getting 5-to-7 pages of script done in two hours is very efficient. How much of this was motivated by the budget?

If we had to do coverage on all those scenes, which means turning the cam-era around and re-lighting, we never could have done City of Hope. *What you find is that there's kind of a geomet-rical progression with any kind of cover-age. Let's say that you shoot the long master and average five takes before you get two or three that you like. If you end up with seven minutes of film and you only did ten takes to get four to six that you will keep, you are way ahead of the game. But if you were going to shoot coverage, with as many as five angles, which is very low for seven minutes of film, and you average five takes per angle, that's still 25 takes. And you still have to worry about matching shots when you get into the editing room.*

Some directors don't like the sway-ing motion of the Steadicam and prefer dolly and track. What are your thoughts on that?

The more people, movement and action in the frame, the less you notice the swaying action of the Steadicam. If the frame is busy it doesn't float as much.

What we tended to do is do lock-offs [the camera comes to a stop] within the Steadicam shot. We don't necessarily want people to be aware that this is a Steadicam shot. What we want them to feel is totally oriented physically.

This raises the issue of the long master versus coverage and cutting. The trend over the last twenty years is to cut faster and come in closer, probably because of the influence of television. The staging in *City of Hope* shows great respect for spatial continuity. Was this a conscious goal of yours in staging the action?

In City of Hope, *we were introducing about 30 characters. Whenever you cut, you disorient the viewer. That's the point of a cut. It disorients the audience enough so that you can give them new information or get rid of time. So one of the things I wanted to do is to orient them in some way, because it was going to be so disorienting to keep track of all those characters. I felt that I should at least orient the viewer geographically. So those long, long takes was a way to counteract what might have been confusing about the first part of the story.*

This also supported the underlying theme of the film which is the intercon-nectedness of the lives of all the diverse characters. Whereas, if we had cut between the various storylines, it becomes even more editorial. It's parallel action rather than linear action. The big Steadicam shots let us create spaces in which peoples' lives cross. But if you're cutting, you end up going from one life to another.

Going to the opposite extreme from the long master, have you found multiple cameras to be useful?

Yes. In the new film, which is set in Louisiana, there's a comedy scene that's kind of a set piece. Two sisters come to visit a woman who's paralyzed and the person who takes care of her. The woman is in a wheel chair. They are sitting out back on a patio. The rhythm of the scene is given by the actors and the cutting, and it's a fairly long scene. There's maybe five-to-six minutes of dialogue between them. So you want to vary the angle. What I find, as an actor in that situation, is that it is very, very difficult to do something over and over and keep it fresh. So that's a situation where I used two cameras not because it was physical action that might not be duplicable, but just that I wanted to reduce the number of times that the

actresses had to do this comedy scene.
We did the two-shot and a single at the
same time. Using multiple cameras
nearly cut the shooting by two-thirds.
And of course your matching is much
better, as well.

STAGING: THE PRODUCTION MANAGER

It is a clear case of bias that a chapter entitled the production manager is written from the director's point of view. But perhaps it is just one more example that film is a director's medium. As any production manager will tell you, his job is to implement, in the day-to-day running of the set, the director's vision of how a screenplay should be shot. The production manager, however, is not paid by the director. He is, in a sense, the director's conscience, if such a thing is possible, and can only tell the director what the men upstairs are thinking. And they are always thinking the same thing: Stay on budget.

Planning a movie production is really an exercise in time management. The producer may talk in terms of the budget, but the actual medium of exchange in commercial moviemaking is the ten-hour day. All the scenes in a script, whether they are one page or ten pages long, must be organized to make the best use of however many ten-hour days are required to shoot the entire film.

The process of commercial moviemaking organizes the scenes, the actors, and all the other resources required to shoot a particular script in such a way that they are used in a concentrated period of time. Therefore, if a Victorian mansion is in the opening shot of a film and appears again at the end of the story, both shots are made on the same day, if possible. Clearly, it makes no sense to bring the cast and crew to a Victorian mansion twice since the production will be charged for a full ten-hour day even if it only takes a portion of that for one shot. Consolidation is the guiding principle in movie scheduling.

Scheduling scenes out of sequence can be quite a complex logistical chore for the production manager. Even in a small picture there are dozens of variables to consider, including: union rules, availability of locations, availability of actors, the time of year, and the artistic requirements of the director.

The principle of grouping resources applies to more than just the consecutive days in the schedule. It also applies to the scheduling of shots on any single day of production. This results in the practice of shooting all the long, medium, and closeup shots with the camera pointed in one direction to take advantage of the lighting setup and then turning the camera around for all the reverse angles.

Apart from special situations, such as action sequences, the most time-consuming part of the staging process is rigging the lights and the camera. Every time the director calls for a new shot, changes have to be made. This can take several minutes or a few hours and it always takes more time than anyone expects. Certain lighting, staging and camera styles require more time than others. If a director is insecure and feels he has to cover every actor in a scene from several angles, it is a certainty that this will require lots of setup time. Another director might feel comfortable shooting the same scene in a single master shot with only a few additional angles for safety. This will probably give him more time to rehearse.

An experienced production manager will be able to make a fairly accurate estimate of how much time any staging style will require for a particular scene. In a sense, every artistic choice the director makes, every piece of special camera equipment, every technique and lighting style has a penalty in time attached to it. As soon as a production manager learns that a crane move is required for a scene, he begins adding time to the schedule. If the crane move is complex, for instance, and must go from a height of ten feet into a tight closeup of an actor's eye, the production manager tacks on another hour. If more demands are added and the actor has to move into position as the crane descends, still more time is added to the schedule.

This, of course, assumes the director gets every request he makes. Actually, the entire process of planning a production is a negotiation between the director, the executive producer, the line producer and the production manager. Much has been written about the lack of artistic support given to directors. While this is a fact of life in the motion picture business, there is another story to be told. Much can be said for the enormous resourcefulness that comes from the successful collaboration between the director, the line producer and the production manager in making the best use of limited resources. If you find that hard to believe, go look at the films of John Sayles.

The production of a movie is not merely a matter of a director battling for more time, more effects and more extras and then waiting for the final decision of the line producer. An experienced director and line producer will avoid this type of conflict by finding alternative ways to achieve their goals. This is true in every aspect of production, from the choice of shooting in right-to-work states like North Carolina, to the selection of an abandoned factory for use as a sound stage.

This is also true of the day-to-day operation of a set and the staging of any scene. A director will have (or should have) a plan for how he will shoot most scenes. If he knows his craft well he can make changes, but even with a new approach he needs to see in his mind's eye an overall view of how individual shots will work together to make a scene.

In a strictly theoretical sense, staging is an abstract problem. Like dance, it sets several elements in motion simultaneously, combining the movement of the actors and the camera. But unlike dance, which is worked out in an open space, filmmakers are encumbered with the logistical problem of complex equipment, and a work day that is full of interruptions. This is further complicated by the practical limitations of shooting on location. The studio environment of the Hollywood classical period made staging considerably easier for directors. Walls, lights, dollies and cranes could be easily moved within the large stages and extra equipment was instantly available.

Any director working on location today who utilizes the conventions of the Hollywood classical style and pushes them to the stylistic limit, will be using production techniques that were developed for the sound stage and do not fit comfortably into a real environment.

Simply put, staging action that requires camera movement and choreography of the actors is far more difficult on location than in a controlled studio environment. If a scene takes place in a relatively small location such as a restaurant or a home, complex staging can be very difficult. It can take several hours to set up a dolly move for a shot that will take only 30 seconds on screen.

This makes it doubly important that the director develop the judgment to predict how a collection of small moments will add up to a meaningful scene.

Of all the staging possibilities available to a director for any scene, the demands of a staging approach must be balanced against many other factors financial and artistic.

INTERVIEW RALPH S. SINGLETON

Ralph S. Singleton is the Emmy Award winning producer of *Cagney and Lacey* and a 20-year veteran producer/production manager/assistant director and former head of Francis Coppola's Zoetrope Studios. His credits include *Taxi Driver, The Conversation, Network, Three Days of the Condor, Pet Semetary, Testament, The Winds of War* (USA) and *Graveyard Shift* which he also directed.

As a producer, what are the things a director should do to get his or her vision of a scene onto the screen?

It's really a matter of organization. Some directors actually put a plan on paper while others keep it in their head. I know of a director who did his own boards, but did not share them with anyone else. Well, it's fine that the director knew what he was doing, but if you don't share your plan with the cameraman and the production designer, it's not very helpful.

What kinds of things can a director do to plan the staging and camera movement for scenes?

Rehearsals are very helpful. Working in an open room with the actors for a couple of weeks before the movie starts to work out all the scenes in the movie, or even to lay out the scene with the actors at some of the locations, is enormously helpful. And not just for the director. The cameraman and the script supervisor should also be at the rehearsal taking notes.

What kinds of things can a director expect to accomplish during the rehearsal?

The director's overall vision for the film and for individual scenes should be ironed out before principal photography begins. And the actors should have worked out the major points of the character with the director at this time.

This allows the director to economize his coverage and to make stylistic choices in the staging and setups. Let's consider a five-page scene of two people sitting around a table talking about life. You know you are going to set a pace for a scene like that. If you are smart, you have laid out a storyboard so you know where you are going to cut into this event [move in with a tighter shot] and when you are going to move out. You shouldn't have to shoot every angle from beginning to end. There is always going to be some overlap of the shots and more angles than you will use. But it's a matter of degree. You can make informed choices to eliminate unnecessary shooting and still be protected with editing options. Rehearsals offer the best time to concentrate on these dramatic choices. That's when you begin to see the story and performance arc. It's very hard to see these things when you are actually shooting.

Don't you begin to see some of these things in dailies?

By then it's too late. You've shot the scene. Besides that, great dailies are one of the most misleading things in the world. Great dailies do not make great films. You sit back and see this wonderful thing and this terrific moment on the screen. But do you have that many moments in the entire film that develop a character or that really have an arc? It's really a matter of not being able to see the overview until the footage is cut together. I've been on some real big pictures that got into the cutting room and then had to go back and reshoot some things or add things to explain what a character was all about. You should have known it beforehand.

You're talking about larger artistic problems than staging. What other areas of a movie can be worked out during rehearsal?

The script. The worst thing you can do is to continue to write and rewrite a script as you are moving forward. It happens a lot. And again, when you are shooting, you don't have an overview. You can rewrite all the way through the shooting schedule and still find yourself in a situation where it just doesn't come together in the editing room.

Is it hard to get the studios to pay for rehearsal time?

Unfortunately, this is usually the case. What happens is that studios are pressed into a situation where they have a docket of movies that they are trying to release. And any of these films costs a fortune. I think the average movie for a major studio costs over 23 million dollars now. And independent films are around 14 million. When you are dealing with those kinds of numbers and you think of the interest on top of that, the quicker the studio gets the movie done and the quicker it gets into the theaters, the sooner they can recover their investment. Knowing this, the studios will say, 'Do you really need two weeks of rehearsal or can you do it in a week?' Or they will say, 'If we give you more time you'll take more time.' Well, they're right and they're wrong. I believe that the longer the prep period is, the more money you will save making the movie. This is because the big money does not get used during prep. It happens when you're shooting. On the film we're working on right now, we know that our average day is 130 thousand dollars. Prep time costs a fraction of that.

How does a director persuade a studio to allow more rehearsal time?

You begin with the actors. Most actors I've met want rehearsal time before the picture begins. They want to have time with the director to talk about the character. They actually want to go to the location, if possible, to see the turf. They want to see where they are going to work. So you already have a built-in interest on the part of the artist. This becomes part of the deal.

When you directed *Graveyard Shift*, you had less than a week of rehearsal. How did you use your time?

We had only four days of rehearsal on that picture. I knew it was a compromise and I had to fight for even that. I had to prioritize my time and work on the key

scenes that needed the most work. I also folded in some rehearsal time on Sundays, after we had begun shooting. But it's still not the same thing as having time to focus on the story without having to worry about production.

What about using extensive coverage so that the director can find the scene in the editing room?

Most editors will ask for a lot of coverage so that they are protected and there are times when this makes perfect sense. But it is also very time-consuming to shoot in 360 degrees, and get angles from every direction. I have seen directors spend an incredible amount of time on a master knowing full well they are going to cover it. By the time they get into coverage, they have spent the actor. And when they get into closeups, where it's really going to count, it's very hard to get the performance.

Are you saying that the staging, and the choice of setups should be respectful of the actor's strengths and limitations?

Yes. It's not just a visual/dramatic choice. You have actors like Nick Nolte who gets it right on the first, second or third take and it's not going to get a lot better than that. Eddie Murphy takes longer to get up to speed. So what do you do when they are in the same scene together? You start with Nick Nolte first and turn your camera around to get Eddie. This lets him warm-up when he's off-camera delivering lines to Nick.

As a production manager and producer, what staging skills do you value in your directors?

Let me answer that this way. When I was on Cagney and Lacey, I worked with a lot of new directors. Television is very good training ground to learn your craft as a director. Usually what I would do with a new director is to say 'Look at all the scenes you have to shoot today and see which ones you can do in a continuous master without losing the dramatic qualities that are needed.' Laying out a continuous master without full coverage is a real art.

Was suggesting a long master shot an aesthetic preference on your part?

No. You want the director to do what is right for the scene. Getting back to Cagney and Lacey, we usually covered seven pages of script a day. A continuous master with reduced coverage saves time. This is important when you are doing television, but ultimately you do what's best for the story. Sometimes a long master is the right choice.

On the other hand, I have also worked with directors who liked loose masters that were so wide that you never got to see the expression of the actors and never caught the moment. So even though we might be getting five pages in one setup we were always outside the action. In that case, a master shot was the wrong choice even though you might be saving time.

But can't a master also incorporate the movement of actors so that the camera frames medium shots and closeups and changes of angle within a continuous shot?

Yes, but this take a great deal of forethought and planning. Forethought to think it up and planning to execute it. You can't do the type of choreography you're talking about without significant collaboration and support from the cameraman and the camera operator and the production designer and everyone else in related departments. Movies are handmade. If you don't plan shots like that in advance, you will end up in *a cut-and-print situation of mediums, OTS' and singles.*

It seems that the staging in the average studio picture today is less well-crafted than the staging in the average studio picture of the 30's and 40's. What has changed?

Again, I think the type of planning that helps clarify the story arc and the director's vision is often missing today. There is a misconception that the time to explore a script is on the set. By the time you are shooting, the time to explore is gone. At twelve thousand dollars an hour, you force the production people and the producing team to be on your case.

What can a director expect to hear from a producer when he begins falling behind schedule?

Hopefully, he doesn't hear silly things like, 'Work faster.' We do say things like, 'Economize your work' or 'Be more intelligent in the way you approach your material.' I think it really gets down to using all the tools that are available, old and new. It could be rehearsals, or storyboards or video taps or specific shot lists — any tool that can be used in a collaborative way so that the major depart-

ment heads are involved in the shaping of the movie. This may sound obvious, but you'd be amazed how many directors resist this process.

Why would a director resist planning his shots with the other departments?

I think it is a fear of losing control of the movie. Some directors believe that by not sharing their ideas in a concrete way until they are on the set, they will eliminate contradictory ideas. Actually, I think the opposite is true. The best way to control a picture and to advance your vision is to use the other creative departments to support a well thought-out plan.

But to be fair, there are a lot of opinions on the set. Everyone feels he can make the movie better than the director.

When a director is talented and prepared, a crew will give him tremendous support. You can't fool the grips and camera operators. After only ten minutes on the set, the crew can tell if a director knows what he is doing.

What about new tools like video taps?

There are a lot of opinions on the set. A crowd always forms around the video tap and comments on each take. It takes time to look at each take and it becomes a second-guessing corner. On my most recent picture we used the video tap to allow the director to monitor the camera view, but we didn't record anything. Overall, however, I think it can be a great tool.

Have you found that it's possible to edit key scenes during the shooting schedule? In other words, editing rough cuts of the dailies on location so the director can get immediate feedback?

You have to consider that the director is working on the set twelve hours a day, six days a week. He sits down every day to look at dailies during lunch time for about 45 minutes. The script supervisor is with him taking notes that are then conveyed to the editor. I'm working on a picture now on location in Texas, while the editor and his team are 1,600 miles away in Los Angeles. They have just enough time to edit the picture according to the director's notes. So the whole delay factor makes it difficult to edit a scene quickly enough for a director to adjust what he's doing. There just isn't enough time. However, I would love to try this with some of the new electronic editing equipment. In principle, what you're suggesting is a good idea.

In all that we have been talking about, the underlying theme is organization as a way of laying the groundwork for effective staging. Would you like to add anything?

I know many directors who have said, 'Well, if I had the opportunity I'd make the movie over again.' Having been a production manager, producer and director I happen to believe that statement is absolutely true. Given the opportunity to go back and do a movie over again, I'd probably do it better. But if I take the opportunity that's out there and use all the various tools, rehearsals, storyboards and any other type of previsualization, then I would have a second chance to make that movie when the picture is shot.

You cannot think that the day you get on the set all the magical things that can happen are going to be there and that you will be inspired and come up with brilliance. It might happen once, or maybe twice, but you cannot be consistent. Because what you have on a movie set is 50 or 60 people and they all have necessary questions that are very distracting to the director. It becomes very *hard for the director to focus exclusively on the story and the performance. The time to focus on style and staging is before you start shooting. You can even change the plan on the set, but you have to work from an organized base that is known to every department.*

part 2
staging: the workshop

3 BASIC CHOREOGRAPHY

In this chapter we'll begin looking at the individual components that make up any fully choreographed scene.

Naturally, the initial factor in the staging of a scene is the logic of the action. Choreography is essentially a matter of choosing between purely naturalistic staging and staging that shapes the drama. How a director balances these factors defines his camera style.

THE SCENE SPACE

A director begins staging by considering the action described in the script. This determines the basic placement of the actors. Beyond basic naturalism there is also a certain degree of dramatic and pictorial license that a director may employ to frame the action.

Theoretically there are an unlimited number of ways to shoot a scene, but only one version will end up on the screen as one staging option after another is pared away for dramatic and visual reasons. If you study enough movies you will discover that there are certain familiar staging patterns. By learning these basic staging strategies a director will be able to more quickly eliminate unworkable staging ideas without having to try them on the set. To put it another way, a director can learn to pre-cut his material. An experienced director does this all the time and it may become so second nature that the director is unaware that he is even doing it.

For choreographed scenes it is useful to reduce the scene space to 3 possibilities shown in Figure 3.1A, B, C. Staging across the frame, In-depth staging and Circular staging. These plans are neces-

3.1A

STAGING ACROSS THE FRAME

sary because of the restricted mobility of the moving camera, but also, because organizing the movement of actors and camera according to a predominant line of motion is a good foundation for complex movement.

3.1B
IN-DEPTH STAGING

3.1C
CIRCULAR STAGING

ZONE AND MAN-ON-MAN STAGINGS

There are two overall approaches to staging that are common in classic movie technique, two ways to think about the way the camera will record action in a single location. We will call these approaches the zone and man-on-man methods of staging. Both stagings are shown in Figure 3.2A, B.

3.2A
ZONE STAGING

3.2B

MAN-ON-MAN STAGING

Examples of zone staging can be found in the opening scenes of *Casablanca* (the first scene at Rick's Cafe) and *The Godfather Part I* (the wedding party). In both cases we are introduced to isolated groups of people or individuals in the same general location. Though it is the different characters that are the subject of each camera setup, the scene is divided into individual spaces each containing one or more of the characters that are at the center of the story. In zone staging the organizational principle of the setups is spatial.

By comparison, man-on-man staging is organized according to the movement of the subjects. In the masterful staging of the action at the party sequence of Renoir's "Rules of the Game" it is the characters that motivate the camera movement within the large interiors of the country château.

To sum up the comparison, zone system stagings structure the shots according to recognizably distinct locations in the scene. In man-on-man stagings the scene is structured around the movement of a subject which in turn determines the spatial organization of the scene. These approaches are not mutually exclusive, in fact, they are usually found together but with one approach predominating.

Both man-on-man and zone stagings, share an underlying technique—they direct the viewer's attention within the frame. This is accomplished by emphasizing particular story elements, transferring attention from one subject to another, determined by the content of the scene but also by the way in which story elements move in and out of view. This can be accomplished by cutting or by choreographing the movement of the actors and the camera. Usually both are used together but in this book we will concentrate on camera and actor choreography.

MOVING THE ACTORS AND THE CAMERA

Specifically, a director has 4 basic techniques at his command when choreographing a scene: static camera shots, moving camera shots, static subjects and moving subjects. They all serve the same purpose: directing the viewer's attention and emphasizing specific story elements.

Beginning with the most basic patterns of movement for actors and camera, here are the basic types of moves.

MOVES FOR EMPHASIS:

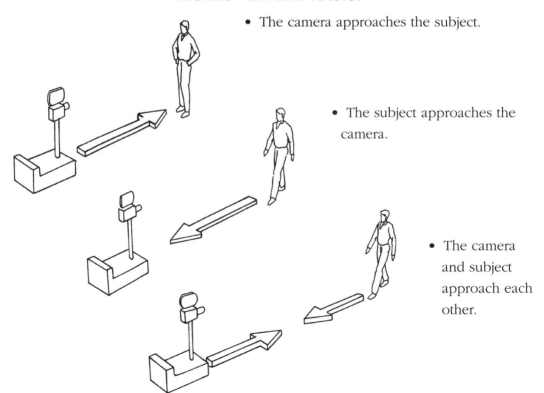

- The camera approaches the subject.

- The subject approaches the camera.

- The camera and subject approach each other.

MOVES TO EMPHASIZE ONE SUBJECT IN A GROUP:

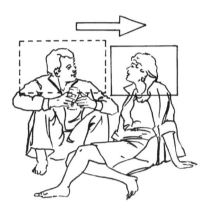

- The camera pans from one subject to another.

- The camera approaches two subjects then moves to isolate one of them.

- Two or more subjects are in the frame, but one of the subjects moves ahead and into a CU.

- A subject turns to face the camera

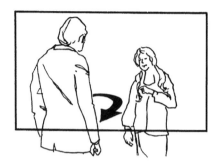 

TRANSFERRING ATTENTION FROM ONE SUBJECT TO ANOTHER:

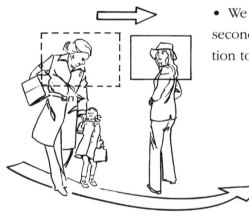

- We follow a subject as she passes a second subject. The camera shifts attention to the second subject.

- The camera pulls back from a CU. to reveal a second subject in the frame.

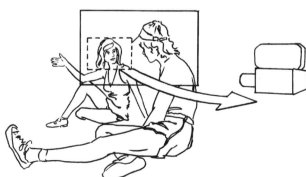

Finally, there is a type of camera movement that joins separate scene spaces or introduces us to scene spaces for the first time.

CONNECTING AND INTRODUCTORY MOVEMENT:

- The camera follows a subject from one space to another.

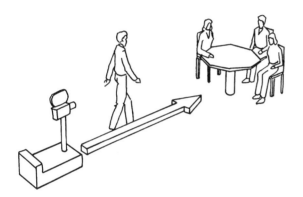

Camera view

- The camera parallels a subject's movement within a single scene space.

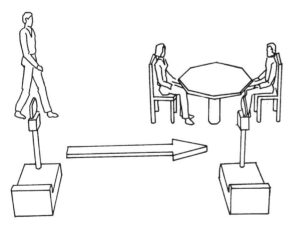

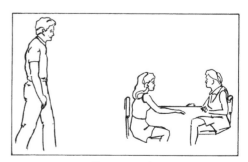

Camera view

COUNTERING

One type of connective move is so valuable that it is worth looking at separately. Countering moves are used to make a major relocation in the scene space or to make a major redirection of the camera view or to cross the line of action. Examples of two types of countering moves are shown below.

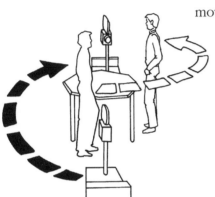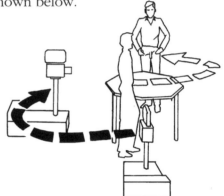

They are called countering moves because they are usually motivated by the movement of a subject in the frame. However, instead of following the same path as the subject, the camera moves in a circular path in the opposite direction.

Countering moves of this type are extremely useful in shifting the camera to a new position in the scene space.

RETRACKING

H. W. Fowler, in his dictionary of *Modern English Usage,* defines elegant variation as the "Labored avoidance of repetition," and calls this one of the most widespread of literary faults. He adds, "The fatal influence is the advice given to young writers never to use the same word twice in a sentence."

In the last two decades a similar fear of repetition has grown up around the movement of the camera over ground previously covered in the same shot—even if the camera is moving in the reverse direction. This is a shame, because retracking is one of the most useful strategies in a filmmaker's staging arsenal. Without it, directors may find that the only other way to reframe the action is by using an unnecessary (an inappropriate) cut. The illustrations below show two stages of a single retracking shot.

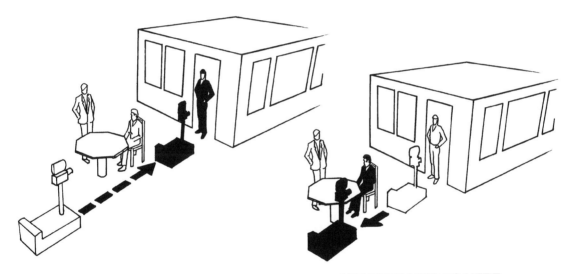

THE CAMERA DOLLYS FORWARD TO HERE. . .

AND RETRACKS TO HERE.

Traditionally, retracking was used for long choreographed shots. This technique is useful when ensemble scenes are played out in a small space, for example, John Huston's *The Maltese Falcon*. Oftentimes the camera will dolly into a position to cover several lines of dialogue and retrack a short distance to a new area of interest, only to return on a third move to the camera's starting point.

LOCATION AND STUDIO STAGING

Staging style is a matter of taste, but it also must fit the practical considerations of production. Of these, no single factor has a greater impact on the choice of lens, camera technique and composition than the choice between a studio or a real location.

The highly choreographed staging style of many of the studio productions of the '30s and '40s is directly related to the absolute freedom to put the camera, dolly and crane arm anywhere in the set. The ability to move walls and ceiling to gain working space or access to cramped scene spaces such as staircases and narrow hallways made '30s and '40s staging technique possible.

Today, real locations are the rule and studio shooting is the exception in the majority of movies. As a result, staging style has been adapted to fit the often cramped interiors of shops, homes and offices. This usually means that much wider lenses are used to obtain common shots such as wide, medium, single and two-shots. It also means eliminating a great deal of camera movement.

Of course using a 24mm wide lens in place of a 50mm lens for an establishing shot produces a very different feel for the scene. It may very well be the lens you would choose for a particular scene, but in a small room it may be the only lens that will capture the shot. The choice for the director is to change the shot or accept the look of the wider lens.

The plan view on the left give you a sense of some of the typical limitations encountered in an average-sized living room (15 × 19 ft.).

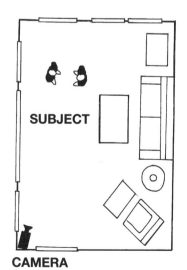

SUBJECT

CAMERA

30MM

35MM

50MM

75MM

The aerial illustration (on the previous page) shows the camera position in the lower left-hand corner of the room aimed at two standing figures. The accompanying camera views show the size of the shot produced by changing the focal length of the lens but not the camera position.

At first it may appear that it is possible to obtain a wide shot with focal lengths right up to 75mm, but if the camera moves in the shot the exaggerated depth effect of the wider lenses becomes apparent and may be undesirable. If the camera is on a dolly or jib arm it is also likely that the camera would have to be positioned even further into the room.

But now consider the problem if the director cuts to a series of alternating OTS shots from the wide two-shot. As you can see in the aerial diagram only a few feet is available behind each player to position the camera. The director would certainly "cheat" the position of the players to give himself extra room, but he would still be forced to use relatively wide lenses to obtain his shots.

The illustration below shows the same room as it would be constructed in a studio set. Any of the walls can be removed to place the camera and dolly at whatever distance is required to accommodate the chosen lens. As you can see, the cameras are placed outside the walls of the room. These positions are typical of camera-to-subject distances for mid-range focal lengths (40mm–70mm).

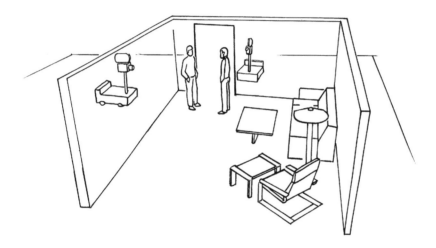

INTERVIEW ALLEN DAVIAU

Allen Daviau, ASC is one of the premiere American cinematographers working today. He has collaborated with top directors on some of the most celebrated feature films of recent times including *The Color Purple, E.T. The Extra-terrestrial, Empire of the Sun, Avalon, Bugsy,* and *The Falcon and the Snowman.*

How do you view your role in creating the look and staging design of a film?

The first job of a cinematographer is to get the director's dream on the screen. The production designer and the cinematographer are the right and left hand of the director and have to get into his or her thought processes. Everyone who works for the director is there, presenting options, telling him, "You could do this ... you could do that" The director will then find a third or fourth way. The director surrounds himself with people who present ideas, but are flexible enough to find a half-way method. Directing is making choices.

You have worked for Steven Spielberg who is known for his highly-choreographed master shots. How do these shots evolve?

Part of his method is to establish the geography of the film's location in the audience's mind. Steven Spielberg does not want the audience to be confused.

He may want to surprise them, but he does not want them to be confused, particularly by geography. In the beginning, one of the reasons for his restless masters is that he takes the audience on a tour—where the drama is going to take place. He can return to that place later and treat it much more elliptically and still not confuse the audience. This is because Steven, for all the flourishes, practices the basics of filmmaking.

Give me an example of how Spielberg would establish the geography for a scene?

Steven likes landmarks. I remember in E.T. at the beginning of the film, when we were at the location for the forest, in the search for E.T., he found these interesting fence poles and later we see Elliot come to the same spot looking for the landing site. And, of course, we are already familiar with it. This is also a John Ford technique—giving the audience instantly identifiable landmarks to help them stay oriented to the location.

Some of the ambitious master shots in Steven Spielberg's movies seem very risky to other filmmakers because so much of the story is dependent on one shot. Is this a problem later if the scene needs to be altered in the editing?

Often Steven will have a master that carries the whole scene, but he'll use a very practical thing, which is a cutaway of someone observing and this is what he and his editor Michael Kahn call a hinge shot. If, for instance, he shoots several takes of a master and the second part of one is better than the second part of some other take, he can cut to someone observing and then resume the master without interrupting the flow. This way he can join the best halves of two different takes. Staying with an uninterrupted master is not as important to him as the energy of the final sequence.

It is well known that Spielberg likes to use storyboards for action sequences, but how useful are they for less kinetic scenes?

Some things he knows he likes to storyboard and other times he doesn't use them at all. E.T. was not storyboarded except for the special effects scenes. Sometimes on a set I can tell he's really

thought it through and he will even describe a detailed shot in preproduction when we are out on a location or on the set. Other times, he doesn't like to be pinned down—he's still thinking about it. I don't think he pre-rehearses very much. The thing he does better than anyone else is, he gets out there and he blocks the camera to the scene and the scene to the camera. The people are moving and the camera is moving. It's very organic the way it develops.

How do the directors you have worked with get coverage?

With some other directors everything is a search. You may wind up going around and around a scene and never really having a master per se, what we call chasing a scene. It may be just as effective for them, but they will not commit to the kind of coverage they are going to do and you shoot a scene in sub masters and closeups. Some filmmakers like John Schlesinger are interested in different things. There you really get full rehearsals with the actors and get everything very well thought out. He gives himself a chance to think about it, he wants his coverage, but, yet, he's also willing to take a chance on masters.

How did you cover a film like *Avalon* where there are dozens of characters and big family scenes?

Barry Levinson is oriented toward capturing the freshest moment of the actors encountering the dialogue. His major approach to a scene is to get coverage that gives him the editorial choices later. He wants to capture the freshest performances of the actors possible. He really does not like to rehearse. He gets the simplest blocking done so we can light a scene and then he likes to roll two cameras and capture the first blush of it. He's always looking for a way to see something that is unexpected.

Does this preclude storyboarding?

Not necessarily. Barry will storyboard many things, but he may radically depart from the boards if he finds something more interesting on the set. He is usually more interested in the CU on the B camera than the A camera master. He uses the master for geography and sometimes he'll use it to establish, but it will then tell him where he wants to go. He's certainly not interested in screen direction. He and his editor, Stu Linder, pride themselves on finding very interesting ways of cutting around the scene that are off-center.

So he finds his scene in the course of shooting it. Avalon *was very complex. You're going around and round a room to find a detail that's going to reveal the soul of the scene. With Barry, you are constantly conducting a search for those revelations. And he wants to do it fast and stay on schedule. The directors who work tend to stay on schedule.*

Steven Spielberg, on the other hand, will find the staging in the master. He will have a blocking rehearsal and at that time I can usually get from him what the coverage is going to be. The cinematographer wants to anticipate coverage so he doesn't trap himself and the director with a lighting plan that doesn't work with subsequent angles. Steven is very, very good at laying out the coverage he has in his mind. And sometimes it will be only a master shot and other times he will cover everything, though this is rare. People are often puzzled on the set because he'll walk away from things without a complete master or CU that really works. But he is very confident about what he's going to do in postproduction and how something is going to cut together.

Interview **51**

How much latitude does this give to the actors?

The actors generally know they are going to have to hit their marks. They understand that the way the scene is blocked is extremely important. Usually, you know that a scene is going to wind up the way that Steven set it.

In *Avalon* you used multiple cameras. Most cinematographers consider this a problematic technique. Do you have the same reservations?

The reason we cinematographers don't like to use multiple cameras is that the lighting will be compromised on one or the other. When you shoot a wide shot, you will make things pop out more by strengthening the contrast. When you come in for closeups, you will soften those contrasts a bit and make them seem a little more natural. When you are shooting two cameras at once, obviously, you have to have a compromise. I've heard that on Rainman, *Barry shot Tom Cruise and Dustin Hoffman's close-ups at the same time. It's a major headache to shoot two camera's together. For Barry it's the way of capturing the freshness of the performance.*

In terms of the shot size and the focal length what is a typical system for shooting multiple cameras?

Well, in Avalon, *you would have the whole scene going on. Barry wants to see the relationships of all the characters one to another but he will have picked the one that is most important to him to cover first. Sometimes you will continue to shoot the master or you might go in to get a submaster on your A camera and then your B camera will go to a different closeup.*

Do you mean that you are repositioning the camera?

Sometimes you start with a wide master and dolly in to a tighter submaster in the course of a scene. Other times, you would shoot the widest wide shot through the scene several times and then Barry will say 'Let's put B camera on this character' and then we go into a submaster with the A camera. And you work your way around the scene and eventually your A camera is shooting closeups and B camera is shooting close-ups. Avalon *not only had big scenes but oftentimes there were children and multiple cameras helps you capture them in coverage that matches.*

Do you find yourself shooting with longer focal length lenses as you push in to get closeups so that A camera won't see B camera?

Absolutely. You get frustrated because suddenly you find yourself shooting a closeup with a 150mm or even a 200mm, when, normally, you would have shot that closeup with a 75mm.

What is your first step when lighting?

I like to get things into position from the beginning. On a rehearsal in an interior, say a day interior, even before the blocking begins I like to have some light coming in through a window. On a night interior I like to have the practical lamps on because I feel something organic happens with actors and the director when there are sources of light present in the room and they tend to block towards them or around them. If you have just a flat overhead work light, no one gets the energy of the lighting. I see actors stage themselves to the light. I started doing this with Steven and we were able to try things with the lighting and Steven may stop and say 'Would this be more effective in silhouette?' And then you go turn out a light and take a look at it. If you wait until the whole

scene is blocked and start lighting, it's a much more complicated process.

What kinds of demands are placed on the Director of Photography and his crew when shooting extensive master shots?

One of the big problems lighting these big masters, for me, is to find a place to put the lighting. When you are working with Steven, you are immediately saying, 'Where am I going to hide the lights, because he is going to explore every inch of the location. Generally, he's very good about that and I will say don't let (an actor) look out that window or don't bring him back through that door. In The Color Purple *I was thrilled with the juke joint set because there were beams to hide lights and the first thing Steven wanted to do was to put people up on the beams so he could look up at them. And in some cases, an extra would have to hide a light with his leg and when the camera moved on the extra, he would have to uncover the light so it could do its job. Sound has the same problem. Steven understands the practicalities, but sometimes he says, 'Just find a way. Because I have to look over there.' ... And you do! He pushes everybody to do* things that they would have thought impossible five minutes before.

What sorts of techniques do you use to hide lights?

Everything. We have lights going on and off with dimmers, lights going in and out on track. In Bugsy, *we had a scene shot in a very small house in a tiny, tiny den. My gaffer had three people working on dimmers, the grips were all floating flags and nets by hand and I was pulling an F/stop change to alter the base exposure to allow a light that was farther away to become the key. And then the F/stop was changed back as the camera moved to a different position so another light takes over.*

When do you get involved in preproduction?

I love to get involved immediately at the very beginning, just when the designer is coming on so that I can sit and talk with the director and the designer when we get into the idea of what the look of the film should be, and at the very earliest location scouts and discussions of sets. I find it's very valuable to be there then and get my oar in. Then I'll go away and do commercials, but I'm available if they need me. I do what I call a split

prep. I do some of my prep in the beginning, go away and then show up occasionally for new locations and finally come on full time five or six weeks before we begin shooting.

On Empire of the Sun, *production designer, Norman Reynolds, and I were standing in an empty field in the south of Spain in November figuring out where the sun was going to rise in May. And Norman was going to build an airstrip there. And you go, 'Gee I hope we were right,' because suddenly buildings are going up. Better you get involved in the planning early, than to come in when it's too late and you say 'Gosh, it's just a shame, but it would have been better if we had built it over here.'*

How much time before you shoot are you able to walk around and get the feel of a big set?

In the practical world, you don't get in very long before you are actually going to shoot. On Bugsy, *we didn't have enough stages so oftentimes we would finish on a set and go out on location while the set was being torn down and replaced by a new set. And then Dennis Gasser would say 'Come on over and take a quick look at the bookie shop.'*

Sometimes you have the luxury of planning things in advance, but there are things like script changes or you lose a location and then you have to adapt. You learn to do things very quickly. The look of a film is a combination of design and discovery.

What are some of the technical characteristics of Spielberg's master shots?

He likes to stage in depth, and he likes to have the camera physically close to the actors. This is not all the time but he does like the depth and dynamic of the wide angle lens.

When you say a wide angle lens, what are we talking about?

Steven used the 17mm an awful lot on Empire of the Sun. *We also used 21 and 24 and 27, but the 17 was very popular for masters.*

E. T. was shot in a narrower aspect ratio, what was the preferred lens for master shots?

On that film we used the 29mm a great deal. It's interesting. He'll sometimes shoot the master with the 35mm and then shoot the closeups with a 21mm lens.

4 BLOCKING IN CONFINED SPACES

There are two types of confined spaces: ones that are in the studio and ones that are on location. Shooting an interior on a sound stage offers far more camera and lighting flexibility than shooting at a real location. This is particularly true for small interiors where your staging options may be few. Shooting a scene that moves around the interior of a real diner, as opposed to one built on a sound stage, may require 50 percent more time to shoot, assuming that you do not modify your staging to fit the limitations of the location.

When there is little space, the most obvious solution is to keep the staging simple and reduce the number of setups. But as it turns out, many directors are forced to be more inventive when they are working in small spaces. For instance, a director may find that shooting through doorways or windows to follow the arrival or departure of a character is necessary to open up a confined space. This, in turn, may produce interesting changes in scale and framing. Conversely, the inability to include the world outside a sound stage diner (except with blue screen or backdrops) may pose a different type of limitation, even though the camera dolly has room to maneuver. This brings us to the paradox that the limitations of confined space often force inventive staging, while the freedom of the studio may encourage directors to use more ordinary staging plans.

CARS, BUSES AND PLANES

At some time in his or her career, a director will probably have to shoot a dialogue scene in a car. Cars, buses, trains and planes represent such special problems that a whole class of rigging equipment has been designed for vehicles of all types.

Car rigging is so specialized that a director should work out any difficult blocking for a car scene well in advance of the shoot day. Unlike a flexible tool like a dolly, which has some freedom of movement even within a small space, a car camera rig is specially set up for a particular type of shot.

Today, there are four basic ways to shoot car interiors. I say today because the fifth way, using insert cars of the kind shot in front of a process screen on a sound stage from the 30's through the early 70's, is rarely used anymore. This leaves the four methods of shooting a real car on location. The first way is to place a camera in the car. Second is to place the camera on the outside of the car and shoot through a window. The third way is to place the camera on a specially designed process car that tows the car that is the subject of the shot. The fourth way is to place a car on a wide trailer that supports the car and a camera on a dolly.

Each of these methods uses special equipment and each has its limitations. Most of the time there is at least some footage shot from a camera placed in the car since this is by the far the simplest camera setup. Illustrations of camera cars and camera rigs are shown on the next two pages.

CAR RIGS

1

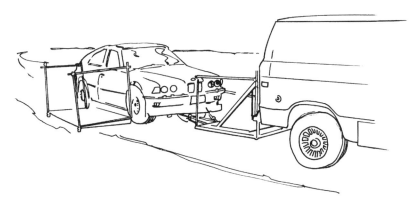

Here is a camera van with a tailgate platform towing a car on a trailer with a lowboy platform attatched to the side. The camera can be placed on the tailgate platform of the van or on the lowboy. Lights are often fixed to scaffold rails on the top of the van.

2

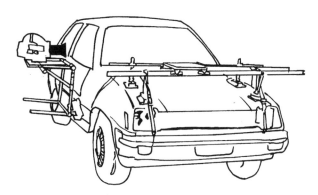

The illustration above shows two rigs: A hostess tray, side door mount with camera attatched and a hood-mounted rail system for fronts shots. The camera can be slid laterally on the front rails to compose the shot. In some cases, two cameras are used simultaneously.

3

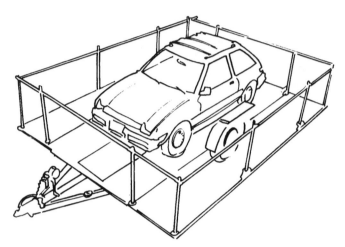

This two-wheel, wide trailer can accomodate a dolly from almost any position around the car. The tracking shots shown in Staging 1 would require this type of car rig.

4

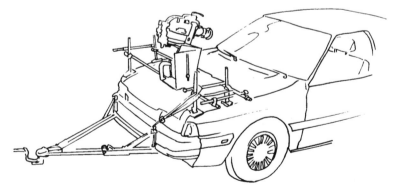

Here is another view of a front-mounted camera. In this case the camera is positioned for a modest down shot. This is a conventional car that has been fitted with a tow bar.

Car rigs and mounts courtesy of Marc Wyler.

STAGING 1 CAR INTERIOR

This staging of a dialogue scene in a car is shot from outside the car with the windows down. On profile, side shots, when the camera is outside the car, it is possible to frame the driver or passenger without including the window frame to enhance the illusion that we are "in" the car. But even when the camera shoots through the windshield from a camera position on the hood, today's audience accepts the convention that we are able to hear the people speaking behind a quarter inch of glass.

In this first version, a process car or trailer is required so that a dolly could be placed alongside the car while it is being carried down the highway. This arrangement gives the director a great deal of flexibility in framing his shots quickly once the rig is set up.

If the shot is framed fairly tight, we will only see a little bit of the window frame, and the fact that the camera is moving alongside the car will not seem unnatural. The advantage of this admittedly complex rig is the simplicity of the setup from a dramatic point of view. It provides a strong sense of spatial continuity (absent from many car scenes) while permitting the actors to work out an entire scene in a single shot or at least in only a few shots.

The version we are about to see angles the camera so that it is looking slightly backwards, but the camera could just as easily favor the front of the car. Depending on the camera lens, the director can get in close to any of the actors or vary the size of the shot.

STAGING 1

1

The camera frames Ann in the back seat through the rear window. We watch her here for some time as she listens to the car radio.

1a

The camera leaves Ann and moves forward to frame the driver and Jack.

D1

Note: To make the diagram clearer the trailer rig has been omitted.

The dolly moves shown in this sequence could only be accomplished with a camera car pulling a trailer carrying the "subject" car with the actors. See illustration 3 on page 60.

D1a

This type of camera car rig permits the use of longer lenses, particularly if this is the position from which the actor on the far side shot of the car is framed.

1b

Ann leans forward into a three-shot. Jack and Ann speak for a few moments.

1c

Ann sits back in the rear seat. The camera follows her.

D1b

It would have been difficult to shoot this scene in a comprehensive master with any other type of rig. The camera can subtly push in or out (zoom) to get in close to a character and this reframing can be hidden during lateral moves.

D1c

The ability to comfortably move the camera into a lower angle, push in or out to a single actor, choreograph the actors into singles, two-shots and three-shots is unique with this camera setup.

ESTIMATED SCHEDULE

Lighting and camera setup time for the process car should be 1 to 2 hours. Camera rehearsal time will also be required to coordinate the dolly moves with the actors. Add an hour for rehearsal. If crew call is 8:00 a.m. then you might not get your first shot until 10:30 a.m. If you're lucky, you might get the shot before lunch at 1:00 p.m. The longer the uninterrupted shot, the greater the chance that something will go wrong.

You'll also have to consider the traffic and road problems. Since the camera is outside the car, it is likely that some framings will include background scenery clearly. If it is necessary to match the background in other shots, then the trailer will have to return to a specified starting point to make the run. This can eat up lots of time. With this particular rig, you can only shoot with the car traveling in one general direction. If you shoot the car on the return trip to the starting point, the sunlight will be on the wrong side of the car and won't match up in the edit.

This is an ambitious shot setup and camera rig, however, if everything goes well, you will have gotten a page or two of script in one shot without setting up for numerous other angles. Some coverage would still be advisable; you will just need less of it. Finally, there is the fall-back position of using the dolly, but only for shooting locked off shots. This allows the director to shoot shorter takes that are less demanding for the actors and easier to cut. It also allows for the possibility that one or two closeup shots could be faked at a later time and inserted into the scene.

TECHNICAL CONSIDERATIONS

With the camera outside of the car, the windows will have to be open to shoot the interior. If any actor has long hair, wind can be a problem. While the director may like the realism of hair whipping around, it may be annoying to the actor. Sound will also have their problems with wind noise. Or, if the day turns out to be hot and humid, you will be stopping every few minutes for makeup to mop up perspiration. I would allow a day to shoot this scene, however, the production manager will want to bundle this with any other shot in or around the car.

With a sequence shot of this type, you can be either a villain or a hero. It is difficult to cut around problems unless potential cutaways are built into the scene. This could be any action; for instance, turning on the car radio (Cut To: a CU of hand on radio) or having an actor look out the window to set up a POV shot. You will probably want to create action of this type at various points in the scene to give yourself cutting options if real problems arise.

Rehearsal is a must. Since camera movement is involved, the director must have real confidence in his camera crew and operator. All the normal problems of shooting a camera move during a long take will be present. Furthermore, you can now add the fact that the car is traveling down an open highway with a camera and a dolly next to it. As you can well imagine, the road surface has to be nearly perfect. Even though a small amount of occasional camera jitter may be realistic, a jolt at the wrong moment can throw the camera operator way off, particularly if he is executing a zoom or dolly at the same time.

If a scene is dramatically troublesome, or the actors have to hit emotional high points such as extreme anger or crying, it might make sense to choose another setup that is simpler. On the other hand, this setup is fairly rare in today's films and is a welcome break from the usual setups that are seen so often on television. The dolly really opens up the possibilities for inventive staging.

Finally, there is the possibility of embellishing the staging by making more elaborate use of the trailer platform. As shown in the storyboard, the camera dollies alongside the car, travelling only about 5 or 6 feet. If a full platform trailer was used (diagram 3 on page 60), the camera could move from a position in front of the car, then travel along the fender and move to one of the windows at the end of the shot. This could be used to introduce the scene or as a pull back shot at the end of the scene.

STAGING 2 CAR INTERIOR

This alternate setup for the scene shown in Staging 1 uses two stationary camera positions, one mounted outside the car on the hood and a second (hand-held) camera inside the car.

With the camera in the car, the director is limited to profile closeup shots unless the actors turn to face each other. This style of staging dialogue is obviously going to rely on cutting to change the viewpoint, but some movement is also possible. For instance, the camera can pan within the interior of the car and zoom in or out on the actors. This is especially useful with the hood-mounted camera since this allows the director to pull back or push in to any of the three actors in the car. This usually works well to begin or end a scene.

One advantage of having the camera in the car is that the director can also obtain low-angle shots. These may be more appropriate to action work, but if the upward angle is slight, it can be a useful angle for a dialogue scene.

For all the thousands of road films that have been made with interior car shots, there is still room for interesting staging in cars. One has only to consider how a closeup stylist, like Sergio Leone, would handle the interior of a car to imagine a whole new range of stagings that could be applied to even the most ordinary car sequence.

STAGING 2

1

The camera begins in CU on the girl and pulls back to a three-shot through the windshield.

Tip: Read through the storyboard first to understand the flow of the shots. Then go back and follow diagrams to find the camera placement.

2

Cut to a CU of the passenger in the front seat. This is taken from an interior camera position on the driver's side of the car.

D1

The camera operator is on the hood of the car and can reframe during the shots. This includes pans and zooms. Reflections off the windshield have become fashionable. In *Annie Hall,* the reflection of palm trees in Beverly Hills passes over Woody framed through the windshield shot.

D2

To obtain this shot, the camera is either rigged on the driver's side of the car or a cameraman is in the driver's seat as the car is towed along. Even when the cameraman is inside the car, special rigging for the lights is usually attached to the outside.

3

Cut to a reverse shot of the driver.

4

Cut to a CU of Ann.

D3

This CU shot is taken from the passenger side. An alternate shot could include Ann in profile in a two-shot with the driver.

D4

This CU shot would certainly be obtained at the same time as Frame 1 to make use of the rigging. CU coverage of the two men in the front seat would also be taken. The cameraman simply has to zoom in on each actor. In this CU shot it is likely that reflections on the windshield would be eliminated by using a polarizing filter and a tent over the windshield.

ESTIMATED SCHEDULE

This is a short scene so it is scheduled to take a half day to shoot. Camera rigging and lighting will take 1-2 hours, but almost certainly the overall setup is simpler than the process car setup required in Staging 1.

Rehearsal time for the camera is minimal. Coordination between the camera and the actors is also much simpler since most of the shots will be taken by a camera operator in the car. (The director will be in the car with the actors or in a trailing car listening to the performance broadcast by radio microphones.)

Matching backgrounds will be somewhat easier because the interior shots will be closeups that do not include significant background information. This also allows for greater latitude if a few shots have to be re-shot later and faked at another time and another place. Not that this is recommended.

The master shot using the hood-mounted camera is shot first. This way the actors get to do the full scene in continuity before moving to the closeups. This will help them shape their performances. Also, if later in the scene the director wants to have the hand-held camera swing around for a look out the window, the rigging will have been removed and won't be in the shot.

While the hand-held camera can be quickly moved around, tweaking the lights will still be necessary. In fact, most of the delays will come from problems other than moving the camera. Makeup, sound, costumes, the actors and traffic will be the cause of many more delays.

Any time the crew members in any of these departments has to make an adjustment, all the cars in the caravan have to stop so that the technicians can get to the actors.

If the crew call is 8:00 a.m. and shooting begins by 10:00 a.m., exterior and interior shooting could be shot in two hours. Taking Murphy's law into consideration, we can add another hour.

TECHNICAL CONSIDERATIONS

Staging 2 is substantially easier than Staging 1. There are three reasons for this. First, is the shooting style which favors cutting instead of long takes. Second, is the use of a hand-held camera in the car for the profile shots. Third, is the hood-rigged camera which is a simpler car setup.

The first and second reasons are related. Using individual CU instead of a continuous master shot is frequently a slower way to shoot than using long takes. However, Staging 2 uses a hand-held camera to obtain medium and closeup shots inside the car and this is a very fast way to shoot the individual setups in the car.

If, however, the camera is mounted outside the car to obtain the profile two-shots of the passengers and driver, this will be much slower than using the hand-held camera. The difference is that you won't be able to obtain the profile two-shot from a hand-held position in the car and will have to substitute closeups instead.

Even though we have considered this shot in terms of cutting, it is also possible to shoot a long master from a camera position in the car. If the director and the actors are resourceful, there are always blocking solutions that can be created with simple pan moves and movement of the actors.

In this staging, there are two ways to get the master. One is with the front shot through the windshield and the second is with the three-way profile shot when the girl leans over the front seat. Since this is a short scene, either shot could carry the scene without cutting to another angle. Would you shoot it that way? While it would seem to represent a considerable savings in time, the truth is that to get this one shot you will be deeply immersed in car rigging and traffic control and there will not be much of a day left to move to a new location for a different kind of scene. You definitely don't want to have to go through car logistics a second time for a reshoot. Therein lies the comfort of coverage. When the continuous master doesn't look good in dailies, what director wants to tell the producer they have to go back? Therefore, it makes sense to get coverage even if a continuous master seems to work by itself.

Another option that should be considered in the scheduling of the scene is the use of multiple cameras. It is possible to shoot both a hood-mounted camera and either a left profile camera or right profile camera simultaneously. Naturally, this ensures continuity of action and dialogue and cuts shooting time in half. It is even possible to use two hood-mounted cameras one for a CU and a second for a two-shot. If location problems look particularly difficult or a challenging performance that is difficult to repeat is expected, a multiple camera solution is worth considering. Since this requires additional cameras and operators, this decision must be made before the day of the shoot.

STAGING 3 BUS INTERIOR

Here is another 3-person staging, this time in a bus. Unlike the car interiors we have just looked at, the camera can be moved within the bus by removing seats to make room for the camera or by using Steadicam.

The following strategies show several angles that are combined within a single moving shot. Generally speaking it is difficult to make cuts within shots of this type which means the director has to get the pacing of this shot just right from beginning to end. One backup method is to design your ambitious master shots to include points at which the camera comes to rest. This makes it possible to cut into them when editing. Naturally, you will want to have an alternate cutting plan in mind so that you can get appropriate coverage. If you plan this well it won't add that much time to the schedule.

Even with a Steadicam it is difficult to move the camera within the bus and it makes sense to choose a principal axis of motion for the camera and to keep the camera path simple. The most logical choice is to move the camera up and down the aisle and to stage the action in depth. The only tricky part of the staging is the fact that we reverse the camera direction at the end of the scene which makes lighting a little more difficult.

In Staging 3 we learn that a stranger is following a woman who is the protagonist of our story. To introduce the stranger and create an ominous mood, the camera will briefly isolate the man as he watches the girl. She is excluded from the shot emphasizing the fact that events beyond her control are taking place.

1

We open on a CU of the woman and pull back to a medium shot ...

1a

The camera pans into the aisle and includes a man seated in the background...

D1

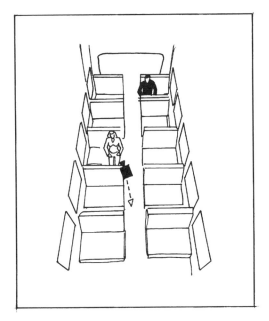

The Steadicam is the easiest way to get a shot with this much movement around the seats. If the rock-steady movement of a dolly is preferred, seats will probably be removed. If a more jittery look is acceptable, the camera can be hand-held.

D1a

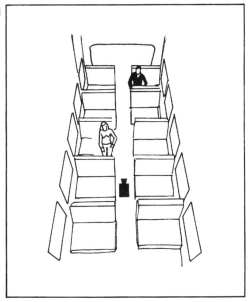

To help smooth out unwanted camera motion a wide angle lens is used. If the spatial feel of a longer lens is necessary a dolly is required.

1b

After a moment at rest, the camera moves down the aisle toward the man and comes to rest when he is in a medium shot. He watches the woman ...

1c

After a few moments, the man stands and the camera backs into the space between the seats. It pans with the man as he begins moving down the aisle.

D1b

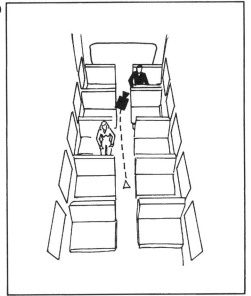

To smooth out the shot, the camera could be over cranked to 30fps. This would not be as noticeable as slow motion, but would make the feel of the shot more deliberate. This is only possible in an MOS shot.

D1c

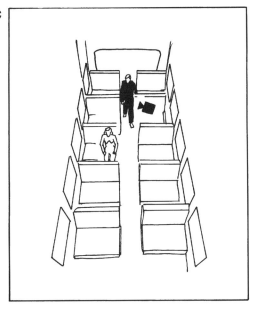

It would probably be possible to move the seats apart an extra foot so that the Steadicam operator could back in between the seats more easily to make the pan.

1d

Continuing the pan, the man has to squeeze by a girl coming down the narrow aisle...

1e

The man sits behind the woman.

D1d

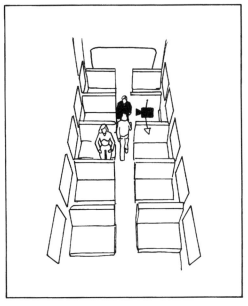

The Steadicam operator might subtly zoom out to a wider shot, hiding the motion of the zoom in the lateral movement of the pan.

D1e

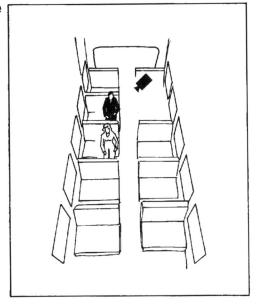

In this diagram the seats have been removed so that the Steadicam operator can back up and frame the man and the woman from the angular rear position shown in the storyboard. Pulling the seats out of the way could be done by grips hidden behind seats while the shot was in progress. In this case, it would make sense to create extremely light prop seats that could be easily moved.

TECHNICAL CONSIDERATIONS

Staging 3 is shot entirely with the Stedicam, a terrific tool that is often misunderstood. The problem arises from the belief that a tracking shot can be gotten more quickly with the Steadicam than with a dolly. But as it turns out, the time-consuming aspects of a tracking shot have more to do with choreographing the actors, lighting and performance than with the laying of track or rehearsing the Steadicam operator. Most of the time, the camera crew is waiting on other departments.

This is not to say that the Steadicam is not very fast for certain types of shots, particularly when it is used in confined spaces such as the bus staging we've been looking at. The only question is whether the look of the Steadicam is right for a tense scene like this one.

One time-consuming aspect of this shot will be the lighting, since we have two closeups and a wide angle of the bus interior all in the same shot. We also do a turnaround at the end of the shot and this would be nearly impossible with a dolly unless the bus were an open set on a sound stage.

In fact, the reverse angle is the type of flourish a director has to give up since it adds considerable difficulty to an already demanding shot.

COVERAGE

Let's consider the type of coverage a director is likely to look for to give himself some options. Since he wants to devote most of his time to his ambitious master shot he would like to get coverage that does not require any major changes in angle.

He will certainly want to get a master wide shot of the action from the front of the bus. He could also obtain various "styled" shots using a longer focal length lens to get in close for detail. These might include a shot that begins on the man's feet as he crosses his legs or moves them impatiently. After a few moments, the camera could tilt up to reveal him in a medium shot as he rises to change seats. A variation of this shot might cover his feet as before, but this time the camera stays with the feet until he moves to the new seat.

Other shots might include a closeup of the woman with a pan and rack focus to the man behind her. A variation might include a pan from the woman in the seat to a passenger passing her down the aisle which transfers us in a second pan to the man. All these shots can be quickly set up from the basic camera position pointing down the aisle. This would be more important if the camera were on a dolly rather than a Steadicam which can move around quickly for locked-off shots. However, even the best Steadicam operator won't be as stable as a tripod and the cameraman would probably put the camera onto a stable platform for some of these shots.

The director will not have to get closeup shots of the man or the woman since they are built into the long master and can be pulled out as individual shots. With these new coverage shots, the story of the scene can still be told by cutting up the long master even though the director prefers the dramatic staging of a continuous master.

Additional protection coverage might include cutaway exterior shots of the bus driving down the road, shots of the other passengers in short cameos and shots out the window of the bus looking down the highway. Generally speaking, a director has a lot of options to cover the action of other people on the bus, weaving them in and out of the central action. It is possible to cut these elements in as generic action, but it makes sense for the director to work out some more specific action in advance. This could be a child who exchanges looks with our protagonist, or a young couple necking in the back of the bus. One thing to keep in mind is that cutaway shots can easily look as though they are simply added on. For this reason, a director might want to try to establish particular extras in the background or foreground early in the scene, so that if he needs to cutaway to them later, the viewer will be familiar with them and they will seem more organically related to the scene. The good thing about elements of this type is that they are mobile and can easily be placed in the frame.

While the scene has been staged to play as one continuous master shot, the director has restricted important action to moments when the camera is stationary, in case the scene must be cut together later on. With this approach and individual shots of action in the bus, the director has several ways to edit the scene.

STAGING 4

Here is a lateral staging of the previous bus scene that uses a third character to motivate camera movement and reveal story elements.

Because it is easier to create open space for the camera when it moves across the bus, it is possible to use plywood flooring for this shot which is less restrictive than dolly track.

As a matter of taste, viewers might object to the lateral move between the seats if the point of view was from the space between seats. This might be seen as an unrealistic vantage point. A more "natural" vantage point is at the very front of the bus, ahead of the first row of seats. It would also help if the camera were shooting with a longer lens so that we are right on top of the seats in the immediate foreground. These might be dropped slightly out of focus so that they are not distracting during the dolly move.

Unlike our previous staging, the story elements are more clearly bound to the dolly moves that precedes the action when the camera comes to rest. This makes it more difficult to break up the sequence later if the director opts to cut up his master. One major reason for this is the fact that the girl and the man are revealed separately. While this helps to build the tension of the scene, the camera move between these characters is necessary to explain that they are seated near each other.

1

We open on the girl looking out the window. The camera slowly begins to dolly right leaving the girl and slowly traveling across the aisle...

1a

The camera comes to rest across the aisle when it has framed a boy leaning over the seat in front of him. The boy stands up and moves left to speak to someone revealing ...

D1

The movement and action of extras in the bus will help hide the movement of the camera.

D1a

As the camera tracks across the frame, the director might want to include a character moving down the aisle to emphasize depth.

1b

... a man in the seat behind him staring in the direction of the girl in the opening shot.

1c

... the boy exits the seat and the camera pans with him...

D1b

Exactly how emphatic the reveal of the man is, can be changed by moving the man one row of seats farther away.

D1c

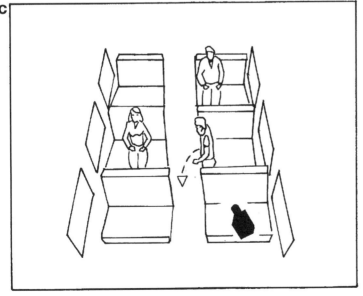

It might turn out that the pan is not sufficiently long, and the director might move the girl forward one row of seats forcing the camera to swing around more to find her.

1d

... until the camera reaches the girl. The camera stays with the girl as the boy exits the frame.

1e

The camera moves in on the girl. After a moment the man sits down behind her.

D1d

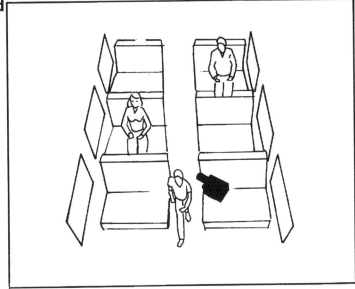

If necessary, the cameraman can hide a slight zoom into the girl during the pan.

D1e

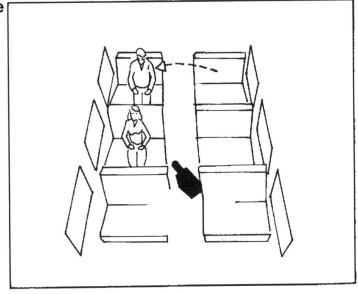

It would probably be necessary to have the camera on a mini jib to get it close to the girl for the final move. Or prop seats that have only backs might be staged in the foreground, allowing more room for the dolly.

ESTIMATED SCHEDULE

This version of the bus staging is somewhat simpler than Staging 3. But there is a tradeoff. In this staging, the seats would have to be removed and executing a dolly shot will probably take more time than the Steadicam shot in Staging 3. The one advantage we have here is that the camera does not turn in a reverse angle at the end of the shot as it did in Staging 3.

Picking up coverage with the dolly will be more difficult than with the Steadicam and even though the camera will probably be placed on a tripod for some of the pickup shots, moving in and around the dolly and rearranging the prop seats will slow things down.

No matter how you look at it, both Staging 3 and Staging 4 will require at least half a day. The production manager would want to shoot the bus near the location of some other scene so that if things go ahead of schedule there will be some other short scene that can be shot.

Since much of the coverage discussed for this staging does not require the principals, a second camera could be used to pick up these shots while the director goes on to another location.

COVERAGE

In Staging 4 we have another instance of a long uninterrupted master that might not work in its entirety. As before, it is imperative that some coverage be shot. But this time it will be more difficult to break up the master. The reason is that the girl and the man are not included in the same frame for most of the shot. In the previous staging we were working in depth and this permitted framings in which the girl was in the foreground and the man was in the background. The viewer knows immediately where both characters are in relationship to each other.

To accomplish the same thing with the lateral setup in Staging 4 means having to shoot the girl in profile with a camera next to her in the seat and the man across the aisle in the background. This is an entirely new setup and one that is far less subtle for introducing the man.

This means that coverage of the story points is more difficult. If we try to assemble the story by using cuts instead of camera movement, we end up with individual shots of the girl and the man. But we don't know where they are in relationship to each other, and any two shots that can be lined up require much more time to set up.

If all else fails, the director could still pick up the shots of other passengers, shots of landscape passing by and shots of the bus driving, as a way of patching the scene together.

TECHNICAL CONSIDERATIONS

Both of the bus stagings are technical stagings. That is, camera movement tells the story. Certainly there are simpler ways to shoot the interior of the bus. Assuming the director insists on this approach, it probably makes sense to tear out several of the bus seats and secure them with some kind of quick release system so they will be safe and stable when driving, but can be easily moved to get various angles. It would also make sense to have prop seat backs available to cheat angles and control foreground elements.

One thing about shooting on buses is that low-angle framings are not as extreme as they would be in a car. This means that a view through the windows shows a great deal of sky. This can be a real advantage since it means the bus doesn't necessarily have to be moving on the road. If the back window is blocked by extras it might be possible to fake the motion of the bus. This will depend on the exact framing of the shots.

It would also make sense for the director to previsualize the scene with a camcorder. This is not the kind of scene that evolves by working with the actors since the story-telling is primarily visual. Certainly a bus interior is easy to simulate in the production offices—a few chairs properly placed will convey the important spatial relation-ships. A director can try all sorts of shots and camera moves and there is even an inexpensive Steadicam Jr. that works with camcorders.

Inexpensive visualization of this type is getting easier all the time as desktop computer-based multimedia solutions appear. For instance, an edited version of the bus scene or any of the other stagings in this book can be put together with a non-linear editing system on the Macin-tosh computer using the Avid editing system or software editing products such as Adobe Premiere. Non-linear means that video footage can be cut together and differ-ent editorial ideas previewed with the same flexibility of word processing with minimal training on the equipment. This is a major advantage over traditional video editing solutions which in the past were simply too time-con-suming and expensive to use for previewing dialogue scenes for film.

STAGING 5

This two-person staging is a good example of how simple movement of the actors and the camera can create compositional and dramatic interest in a simple location.

Included in this brief scene are most of the basic staging strategies that we will see throughout the book. Relocating the action, actors moving to the camera, obtaining reverses by turning an actor to camera, leading the camera into the scene space and countering movement are all used to tell the story. While this may sound like a lot of choreography, the scene appears simple when viewed, because all the action is confined to two areas. The point is that if the geography of the scene is clear, changes of angle and the repositioning of the actors within the frame, can be used without fear of "over directing" the scene.

Above all, notice the respect for frontality. We do not use the shot, reverse shot pattern in many instances where it would be expected. Instead, movement within the scene space is accomplished by creating two basic camera directions or zones and only using reverse shots in the second space after it has been established.

The two frontal zones form an L shape (see page 113) and are connected by the movement of the woman in panel 2b when she repositions herself in the scene. The camera follows her, thereby establishing the new space.

The scene takes place in a gazebo. The camera picks up the scene as the man arrives at the gazebo to meet the woman. Dialogue has been added to help give a sense of motivation to the staging and editing pattern.

1

The first shot is a wide shot. Carl approaches the camera, turns screen right and heads up the stairs...

1a

The camera dollies forward, turning right and craning up to the gazebo paralleling Carl...

D1

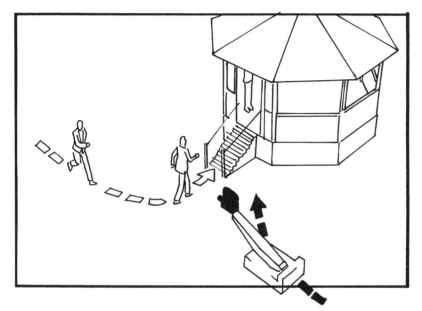

This shot would be photographed with a small crane or a jib arm on a dolly. The move would start very slowly probably beginning as a parallel dolly move for a moment before craning up.

D1a

As we begin to include Jean in the shot, the camera operator has the option of favoring Jean in the shot rather than Carl.

1b

.. .Carl comes up to Jean. The camera follows...

1c

... The camera move ends in a two-shot of the couple.

CARL: I wasn't sure you'd be here.

JEAN: That's me. Old faithful.

D1b

As storyboarded, Carl gets ahead of the camera so that he is seen in low angle going up the stairs, but this is a matter of taste. The camera could easily get ahead of him and frame Jean, only to have Carl reenter the shot a moment later.

2

Cut to: A wide OTS of Carl.

CARL: Do I have to tell you it's appreciated?

2a

Jean turns away.

JEAN: I'm not looking for appreciation. If you want to appreciate something go to the Louvre.

D2

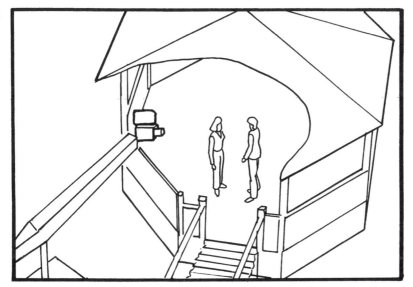

Since we are going to move the camera in this shot we will stay on the crane. This means clearing the ground around the gazebo and laying down track or plywood.

D2a

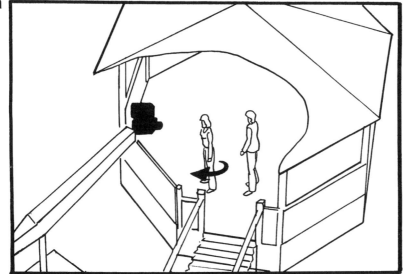

In a shot like this it is not uncommon to have the foreground figure step closer to the camera for an ECU.

2b

... Pan with Jean as she turns away from the camera and walks at a right angle to the railing. The camera follows her by dollying forward a few feet. She turns back to face Carl.

3

Cut to: Carl in medium shot.

CARL: I didn't come here to fight.

D2b

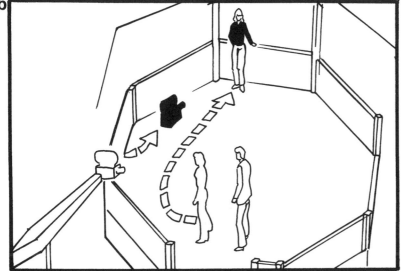

Generally speaking, pans, dollies and cranes can be combined, but it is often the case in non-action sequences that moves are broken down into segments, however short. In frame 2b the move would be—pull back 2 feet.—Pan 90 degrees—dolly forward 5 feet. Naturally, the operator would strive to tie this together seamlessly. The whole move might last only 8-10 seconds.

D3

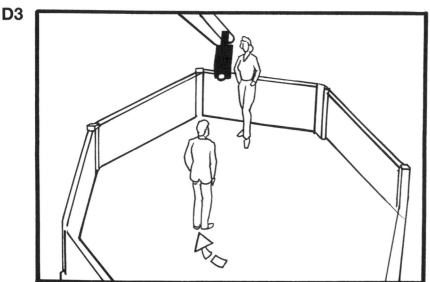

Even though these are locked-off, medium shots, it might be just as easy to leave the camera on the crane as to set up a tripod.

4

Cut to: Jean in a reverse medium shot.

JEAN: Why did you come? I'd really like to know.

5

Cut to: Carl, in a repeat of frame 3, only now he steps forward closer to the camera.

CARL: I'm here because you're my business partner and a friend.

D4

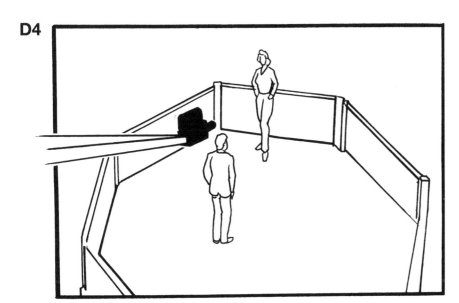

In this and the following medium shots the camera is locked-off, but the director would probably cover them in different shot sizes and possibly OTS shots.

D5

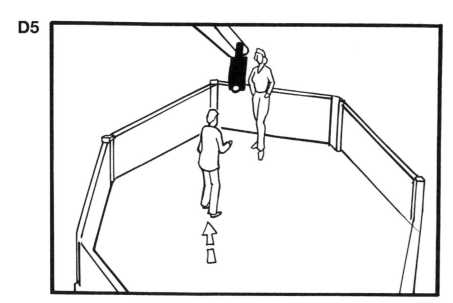

This basic and useful device in which the actor steps closer to the camera is a good way to emphasize a line of dialogue or the growing interest of a character.

6

Cut to: Jean in a repeat of frame 4.

JEAN: That's what I thought you would say. You might as well know—I've gone to an attorney.

7

Cut to: Same frame as 5...

D6

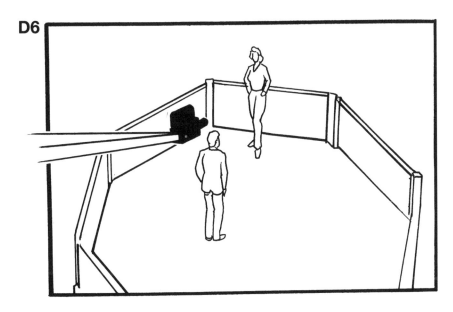

We repeat the reverse shots and although we only show one camera, the angle would permit us to shoot both shots simultaneously with two cameras or to get a closeup shot and medium shot of either actor.

D7

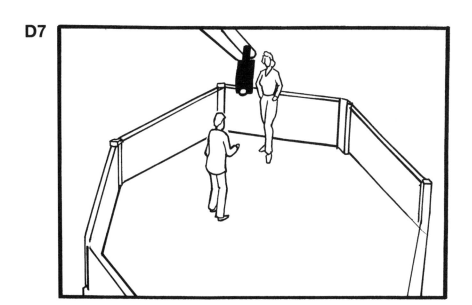

7a

... Carl steps into a profile two-shot and the camera pans with him. The camera comes to rest as they speak.

CARL: You called an attorney? That's great. You know if I declare bankruptcy you go down with me.

JEAN: I don't even care anymore.

7b

Jean walks around Carl to leave... The camera begins to move again.

D7a

This first pan move is separated from the next move in D7b by several seconds. Another option with this shot is to dolly the camera in closer for a tighter profile two-shot.

D7b

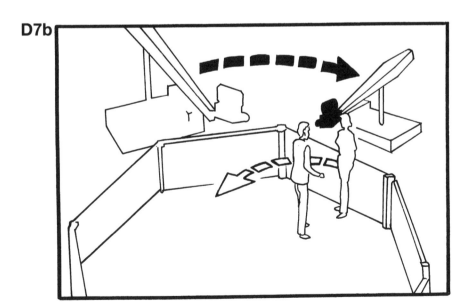

This is almost a counter move in that the camera moves around just short of a quarter turn to include Jean as she leaves.

7c

.. .We stay with Carl who steps forward to the camera as Jean exits in the background.

Figure 1 on the opposite page shows the general blocking areas used in Staging 5. The broken lines indicate the line of action for each area. We make the transition from one area to another when the girl repositions herself from the area closest to the stair to the second staging area at the top of the illustration.

If you go back and look at the storyboards you will notice that in D1, the camera is on the right side of the line of action. However, when the new space is established, the camera shoots from the left side of the line. This arrangement avoids bringing the two actors across the frame when the girl moves to the new zone. If for any reason, it became necessary to cross the line, it can be accomplished by having the man cross during the shot, preferably when he is in the foreground.

D7c

The meaning of the scene changes depending on which of the characters we favor in the frame at the end of the shot. As shown in the storyboard, we favor Carl who would probably step closer to the camera for emphasis just before the transition to the next scene.

Figure 1.

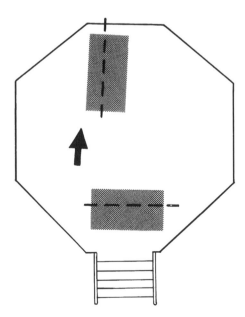

ESTIMATED SCHEDULE

The director arrives on the set at 7:00 a.m. and greets the DP and the production manager. They have previously walked through the scene on a location scout, but the director has thought of some changes since then. The creative team roughs out the scene one more time.

The only significant change the director requires, is to make the opening shot a continuous move. Since the director wants to view the approach of the man in a relatively low angle, and then move into an eye-level two-shot of the man and woman on the gazebo (which is raised), the camera will have to be elevated with a jib arm or crane.

Now the director, production manager and DP discuss the order in which the shots will be photographed. It is clear that there are three moving shots with re-framing, camera movement and choreography. These lead to a pair of medium shots in the shot, reverse shot pattern. The director wants these in a variety of framings. He also has two ways of staging the ending counter shot and wants both of them. He will make the final decision about which one to use in the cutting room.

With this information, this is how the assistant director breaks down the scene:

First the opening shot 1-1c. Since this will establish the basic orientation of the scene, everyone agrees they should get this out of the way first.

At the end of this shot, the camera can be moved into position to get shot 2-2b. At the end of this shot, we are also in position to get all the girl's medium shots and CU shots which include all the dialogue and reaction shots from 3-7.

Now we can reverse the camera and get all the man's medium shots and reactions for this same section, shots 3-7. Since the dialogue is short, the director will let the scene play through this entire section including the camera move 7-7a.

The last shot on the schedule also happens to be the closing shot of the scene (7-7c). The director agrees to this plan since it very nearly follows the sequence of the script.

This is almost certainly a full-day shoot.

TECHNICAL CONSIDERATIONS

Since we are outside, the weather is definitely going to be a consideration. Even though the gazebo is covered, any rain can kill the shot. If the weather goes bad and looks like it will stay that way, the director should have a backup plan to speed up the shooting. This means eliminating some of the camera movement.

Since the camera gets into a profile two-shot early on and allows the girl to turn to the camera, this overall strategy could be used to shoot the entire scene. Naturally, the director could let the man move, to add interest, while restricting action to this general framing.

The choice of having the girl move to establish the new scene space is what adds interest to the staging, but it is also a choice that adds quite a bit of time to the schedule. This decision means reversing the scene space with the consequent changes in lighting and repositioning of the camera.

While it may seem that the crane might add time, this is not necessarily the case. Actually, the crane can be moved outdoors fairly easily, and the moves are not particularly complex. Most likely there will be other delays for costume and makeup that will exceed the time necessary to move the dolly and crane. In fact, the crane might help speed up production since it can reach several areas of the set without having to move the dolly track.

Finally, there is the option of using multiple cameras. While the diagrams for Staging 5 show only a single camera scheme, it is certainly possible to shoot with two cameras. The shot, reverse shot pattern used to get the medium shots in frames 4, 5, 6 and 7 could be photographed with two cameras, while other dual camera setups could be used in conjunction with the moving camera to pick up coverage. One must always consider, however, that multiple cameras can get in the way of moving shots and complex choreography. As storyboarded, Staging 5 would not benefit from a multiple camera set up as well as scenes which are demanding for the actors or which involve larger casts and extensive coverage.

INTERVIEW DUSTIN SMITH

Dustin "Dusty" Smith has been a grip in the motion picture business for more than 20 years. He has worked with many of the best directors and cinematographers in the business and is considered a specialist as a car rigger.

What are some of the pitfalls when doing a car shot?

It is almost always dangerous for everyone involved, including talent. It is often restricted by forces beyond anyone's control; i.e., traffic, onlookers, bicyclists and so on. In a calm, driving scene [not a car chase], you can use up your designated mile of road before you've even got two takes. You can't turn around and start again. You have to turn around, go all the way back, turn around again, and then invariably wait for makeup and such to do everything all over before you can make a second run.

What kind of matching problems should you be aware of?

In my early days as a grip, I rigged a car to be driven by Don Murray on New York City side-streets. We spent a whole afternoon shooting a difficult dialogue scene from the hood. The mounted cameras were as stable as rocks, the D.P. was happy and I was happy. But the next

day, after dailies, the D.P. wouldn't talk to me. All the side shots looked like we were going twice as fast as the front-mounted shots. Although, technically, this was not my responsibility, it is a lesson I learned the hard way. The rule of thumb is that the speed of the car in side shots has to be shot at 30–40% slower speeds than the speed in shots photographed from the front.

What other illusions have to be created when shooting car shots?

One problem directors always miss is this: The actor is told by the grip not to force the steering wheel, to let it do the turning [the car is being towed]. The actor should hold the wheel lightly. Serious problems can result with the hitch if the actor were to do otherwise.

Yet another mistake, I think, is the blind insistence on rock-steady cameras. This, too, can give the appearance of a process shot—something that must be discouraging after paying for the time and effort to do it for real.

In Staging 2, we have a side-mounted camera. What lens do you normally use to have enough depth-of-field to hold the driver and the passenger in the front seat in focus?

What you usually do is pull [cheat] the passenger seat back a little so you can see the driver. The camera is placed on a hostess tray [a camera platform], usually with a 24-35mm lens.

In Staging 1, we move alongside the car with a dolly shot. How would you rig that?

The way you would do that is to shoot on a very low trailer called a low boy. When you pull the car on the trailer, you sometimes deflate the tires or even take them off and set the car as low as possible. That way, the camera car is fairly close to the height it would be if it were on the road.

If there is dolly track, you will need a wide-body, process trailer. You would want to use a small dolly, like an Elemack, where the operator can be very contained. Of course, with any dolly on a track, if the tow vehicle puts on the brakes quickly, the dolly flies forward. So, if the car is moving, it would be better to use a dolly with a braking system,

like a Fisher 10. Anytime the car is in motion, any kind of acceleration or de-acceleration makes a camera-move very hard to control.

How much time is involved in setting up a hood-mounted camera?

For the initial setup it takes about an hour. But you really have to consider the overall rigging job. You have three elements: camera, sound and lighting. Since what you are doing depends on the weather, you never know exactly what the requirements are going to be. If you have sun and glare off the windshield, you have to put black above the glass to cut reflection and that's difficult to rig. The actual hood mount goes on fairly quickly. You can move it around, push it in or move it left or right and there are a lot of good rigs for this. The same is true for side-mounted cameras, only this is a little bit slower because car doors have to be secured. But overall, your delays are not caused by the mounting of the camera.

Where do you put the lights?

The lights are usually rigged from a roof rack or set on the towing vehicle, itself. Most of your time is taken up securing cables alongside of the car and having the sound people or the lighting people get under the dashboard, which means that the talent has to get out of the car for adjustments. On average, you can expect an hour per setup [camera angle].

What are the factors that have to be considered choosing the route that the car follows?

Well, you have to match the background and the sun. You can't shoot driving North and then turn around and shoot coming back South on the same road. Or, you go for a long, long run if you are out in the country. The same thing if you are shooting a train. Obviously, you don't want just to back the train up every take—you want to keep on going. A train is double the problem of a car.

How many cars are usually in the caravan?

That can vary greatly but you will usually have at least four or five. This includes a van full of the makeup, wardrobe and props people and their assistants. Then you have the camera crew in the towing car. There will be a grip truck with equipment and secondary crew members. There will also be a trailing car with a professional driver and the police vehicles. The number

of cars increases with the complexity of the shot. Also, there will probably be some kind of food and equipment trucks at the staging area that don't follow the camera car for the shot.

How does the director communicate with the actors?

He's almost always in the back of the towing vehicle elevated up so he can look down through the windshield of the car with the actors. He's listening to the dialogue on headphones and communicating with walkie talkies. The assistant director is right next to him. He would probably be telling the driver to go faster or slower but the key grip would be responsible for pulling the plug if he saw something up ahead on the road he didn't like. Or, if things were going too fast for safety.

What's the general rule for matching the speed of a profile shot with the speed of a front shot?

Let's say you were going 25 miles an hour and looking through the window. That would be your base speed. If you side mounted the camera for a profile shot and you were going 25 miles, it would appear nearly twice as fast or at least substantially faster. So, if you shoot *your side-mounted shots at around 50 or 70% of the speed of a front shot, then you would be in the right range to match the shots later.*

What is a typical base speed for dialogue scenes in cars that are not action scenes?

25 or 30 miles an hour is a comfortable driving speed. And it looks comfortable. As long as the other traffic isn't passing you by, a scene in a 55 mile per hour speed zone looks acceptable to the viewer if the camera car is actually doing 30 miles per hour.

If you have a really big scene that includes shots outside the car on the highway or if you include shots of the characters in the scene looking out the window, how do you control the environment outside?

Any traffic seen outside the car that interacts in the slightest way in the shot has to be driven by professional drivers on walkie talkies. The key grip has to plan that all out. People pull up all the time and have interesting things to say, like "Put me in the movies or How do I look?"

What about the safety factor? For instance, you rarely see passengers wearing seat belts in the movies.

A lot of directors don't want the talent to wear shoulder harnesses. You also have to consider that the crew is hanging out of the back of a car, and even though they are secured, they are still unprotected.

Who is leading the caravan?

Police are at the front with the lights going. But the best way to do a car shot is to find a stretch of road and own it. You used to find places outside the cities that were perfectly happy to shut down a road for a movie because they were so enamored of the business. But this is becoming less and less the case.

What about a bigger vehicle like a bus? Can this be towed?

You can tow anything. If it were necessary, you can put a semi on a semi. You might do that with a bus if the sound in the bus was a problem. But the shot, and its importance dramatically, has to justify all the effort. You would find a simpler way to shoot a scene like that unless you had a really big scene in the bus and even then you might want to simplify your setup.

What about the new super towing vehicles like the ShotMaker?

That's a beautiful vehicle and you can do all sorts of things with it. It has a crane and I suppose if you put a remote head like a Hot Head on it you would have a safer way to do shots that would normally have an operator out on top of the crane.

Compare the degree of difficulty of a dolly move during a dialogue scene of people walking versus a car scene?

Car shooting is just plain difficult to control. In any scene you can make the camera work as difficult as you want, but all things being equal, car shooting is probably the most time consuming of locations excluding effects sequences.

Also, equipment for doing straight-ahead tracking shots has improved a great deal. Track goes down very quickly, and with the new sled systems [track on wheels that offers very smooth operation] you can move the track around very easily. Frankly, the delays during a tracking shot in a dialogue scene often have more to do with makeup, perfor-

mance and decision-making than with the actual mechanics of laying track and rigging the dolly.

At the end of the interview on car setups with Dustin Smith, we spoke about the general operation of the set from the grip's point of view. When I asked him to describe the best method he had seen over the years for organizing the staging and rigging of the set, he sent me the following list.

1) Clear the set completely for actors and director. Send the crew away, stop the moving of sets, QUIET.

2) Once the blocking is complete, call in only the relevant department heads, (Script, Gaffer, Key Grip, Dolly Grip, Set Dresser, A.D.'s, and stand-ins). Rehearse the principals for marks and moves.

3) Clear the set of principals and director.

4) Give the set to the crew and stand-ins only.

5) Call in the principals and their support crew for final rehearsals.

6) Shoot.

ADVANCED CHOREOGRAPHY IN CONFINED SPACES

In this chapter we will be looking at stagings that use long, continuous camera movements to cover multiple story points. Of course, story points are covered in the dialogue, but they can also be presented visually with physical action, props, POV shots, reaction shots and the entrances and exits of characters. Generally speaking, a sequence shot of this type takes the separate elements that would appear in the individual panels in a story-board and combines them in a single shot. This is done by bringing new story points into the shot with camera movements such as pan or tracking shots and by moving the actors within the frame.

How do you choreograph long master shots of this type? One way to begin is to make a list of the story elements in a scene or to create a storyboard of the action with one storyboard panel for each story point in the scene. Your next job is to see how to combine the information in any two panels into a single panel or shot. For example, a CU of a diary on a table + a medium shot of a man standing near the table = a single deep focus shot of the diary in the foreground and the man in the background. The connection between these separate elements could just as easily be a pan or dolly move.

Directors who are comfortable designing sequence shots generally have a wide vocabulary of cinematic devices that they can call upon for any situation. In addition to knowing specific techniques, it is also useful to have a healthy appreciation of indirect framing. For instance, allowing principal subjects to carry dramatic passages while far away from the camera is a useful strategy.

If there is an underlying strategy behind successful sequence shots, it is the repositioning of the actors to minimize camera movement. Extensive camera movement of the type used by Orson Welles in the bravura opening of a *Touch of Evil* is the exception. In this famous sequence the camera movement was justified because the scene was set outdoors with the action covering several blocks of city streets. But many of today's directors will use the same type of liberal camera movement when it is actually easier to reposition the actors to reveal story information. Learning to move the actors to the camera is perhaps the most important staging skill that a director can develop.

With that in mind here are some thoughts on balancing camera movement and the movement of the actors: First, the camera can move to large areas of a location which sets up the specific choreography of the actors within the general space. This was demonstrated in the previous chapter in Staging 5 when the camera moved between two basic zones in which the actors' movement or cutting was used to vary the viewpoint.

Another strategy has the camera moving laterally or in-depth within a single space moving between the actors. To put it even more directly, the camera can cover the geography of the scene while changes in shot size and subject can be controlled by moving the actors within the frame. This overstates the case somewhat since the camera can very effectively select individual subjects in the frame, however, this is a use of the camera that is practiced and understood far better than choreography of the actors.

STAGING 6

This next scene follows a police detective who is pressuring a teenager into admitting his guilt for an unspecified crime. The detective uses all his persuasive methods as an interrogator to manipulate the boy, and this becomes the central dramatic action which motivates the camera movement. A continuous shot is the appropriate technique to use because the detective's monologue is intended to be hypnotic. If we were to use extensive cutting instead of the continuous shot, it would diminish the effect of the detective's speech.

The majority of the scene has been staged using three long, in-depth camera moves that follow the same general line of action. In the final version the director might choose to eliminate one of the long moves, and substitute one or more locked-off coverage shots to change the pace. It would even be possible to combine the three separate camera moves into one long take. This option is available because the camera path and the lighting remain pretty much the same for all three shots.

In addition to the tracking movement, the camera cranes down on a jib arm to frame the confession and to get a low angle view of the detective. This is a good example of how various story points (the detective, the teenager, and the confession) can be placed within the scene space to motivate the movement of the camera and the dramatic arc of the scene. For example, moving far away and then back in close to the teenager, follows the rise and fall of tension better than a lateral camera move.

1

We begin in a ECU of a boy being interrogated by the police. We hear the O.S. voice of an officer reading out a confession in a monotone. The camera pulls back slowly into...

1a

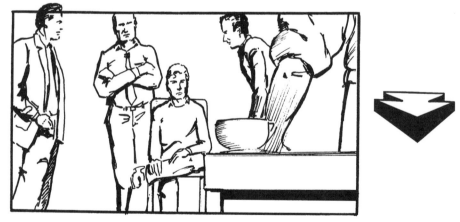

... a wide shot of the four policemen surrounding the boy. The camera continues to dolly back and to the left...

D1

This is such a long move that the director would almost certainly add the movement of one of the policemen to break up the shot...

D1a

Most likely one of the detectives would come forward and exit the shot or come forward and take a cup of coffee.

1b

... the pull back continues. The camera simultaneously moves left framing a police stenographer reading from a confession that is in a typewriter.

2

Cut to: A medium shot of the teenager. One detective moves slowly around him as he begins to speak. The camera begins to move in a clockwise semi-circle pulling back at the same time...

DETECTIVE: Your friend turned you in. We have it all here in black and white.

D1b

The camera would probably pick up the cop reading from the confession in medium shot and then move back into him during the move left. Again, the movement of other cops in the room might be added to cross the frame.

D2

Once a move of this type has been set up, it is fairly easy to change the opening framing. For instance, the director might get one version that starts on the teenager and a second version that starts on the detective.

2a

.. .The interrogator begins to move forward slowly, speaking as he walks. The camera backs up ahead of him as he moves into a CU...

DETECTIVE: The thing about doing time is how everyone on the outside passes you by.

2b

.. .The detective stops at the stenographer's desk.

DETECTIVE: That girlfriend of yours— Are you sure she's just going to sit around for six years while you're in the can?

D2a

As the move continues, the camera dollies left while backing up. This keeps the teenager framed in the background.

D2b

The camera booms down and tilts up to the detective before he reaches the desk. When the detective stops, the camera move stops.

2c

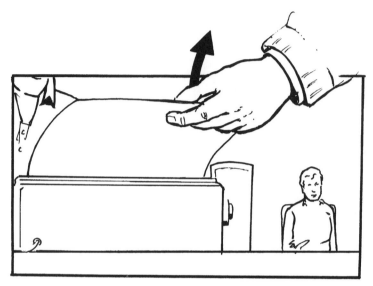

... The detective steps out of frame on the right side taking the confession out of the typewriter.

3

Cut To: A medium two-shot.

D2c

The camera swings around to frame the boy in the background. The confession wipes the frame as it is removed from the frame.

D3

The wipe on the previous shot sets up this new shot. The director would also get separate medium shots of the boy and the officer in the vest as alternatives.

4

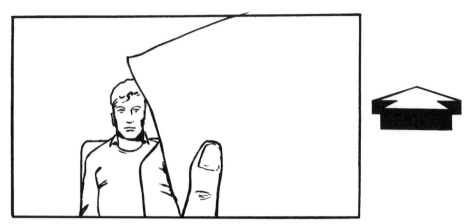

Cut to: A CU shot of the "confession" held by the detective. It's a blank sheet of paper. He moves the confession a little to the right, revealing the boy. The detective moves forward and the camera moves with him...

DETECTIVE: We have enough here to put you away right now. But that means a long trial—

4a

.. .The camera dollies forward to the boy as the confession slips out of the frame...

DETECTIVE: If you help us, this thing can go a whole lot easier--

D4

The camera operator would have to rack focus from the paper to the teenager.

D4a

The director might want to include the detective as a framing device on the right side of the frame as the camera tilts down to the boy.

4b

...The camera tilts and begins to boom down moving in closer on the boy.

DETECTIVE: Right now we're the only ones looking out for you.

4c

The camera ends in a very tight CU of the boy.

D4b

We have changed dollies in this diagram even though it is a continuous shot. Actually this shot could be done as a zoom or as indicated here, a camera move using a boom.

D4c

Another alternative is to boom up slightly while zooming in on the boy to get the perspective-shift *"Vertigo"* effect invented by Hitchock and popularized by Spielberg in *Jaws.*

ESTIMATED SCHEDULE

Even though sequence shots are highly choreographed and require precise execution, they are often flexible enough to allow for different versions. This is largely made possible by panning the camera on the dolly. For example, once a pull back move from a seated figure is rehearsed, a camera operator can start in close up on anything within the range of the camera and pan to any other object nearby. This means you can have different opening or closing frames for any dolly move. If a director plans for this in advance, he can give himself extra cutting options. Naturally, this means that sequence shots have the potential for eating up extra time, the same as shooting every conceivable angle for coverage.

In Staging 6 we'll assume that the storyboard was followed fairly closely for a feature film. In that case the sequence shots could be shot in three quarters of a day or about seven hours. A weekly, one-hour television drama wouldn't have the time to shoot in this style unless the moves were simplified and shot with a Steadicam. This would give the scene a different feel. Additional coverage would probably use up the rest of the day.

When working on a tight schedule, the director is well advised to have a a simpler staging all ready to go. If the director, continuity person, storyboard artist and cinematographer are in sync, it is possible to create a shooting plan that is like the bulkheads in a ship; even if part of one long dolly shot doesn't work, the rest can be salvaged. This means finding the points in the continuous shot where cutaways are possible. Some directors create the storyboard in preproduction and think that this type of protection coverage is something that can be figured out on the set. Frankly, the kind of ingenuity it takes to create alternative cutting patterns that make efficient use of the production resources can take days to figure out.

In the interest of getting the most work done on a limited schedule without giving up the sequence shot, pre-shooting the scene with a camcorder would be very useful. This shot could easily be worked out on a rehearsal stage during preproduction. But even shooting a version on the set the day of the shoot could help the director determine the exact choreograpy he would like to select as the master. This can be done with a video tap using stand-ins or with a camcorder if the dolly track has not yet been put down.

COVERAGE

Coverage for Staging 6 offers many possibilities since there are several characters in the scene. There are opportunities for reaction shots of the other officers, which could include medium shots, two-shots and close-ups, as well as closeup shots of the sweaty hands of the teenager, and wide shots of the entire interrogation room.

As in other scenes we have looked at, the director will want to keep a list of slice-of-life behavior that will comment on the scene. For example, the director might want to include some repetitive sound like a coffee machine operating that is grating on the nerves of the teenager. This motivates a shot of the coffee machine. Or the teenager may be trying to shut the whole scene out by counting the cracks in the floor. This sets up a whole series of shots that includes the teenager and POV shots of the floor. If these ideas are worked out carefully in advance, some of the shots might be picked up by a light crew working with the cinematographer after the production manager has taken some of the actors and crew off the clock at the end of the day.

TECHNICAL CONSIDERATIONS

Overall, the second and third camera moves are reasonably difficult, combining craning and tilting moves while the detective is speaking his lines. Another aspect of the moving shots that may create problems is the fact that the moving shots involve closeup work. This makes focusing the camera a problem for the operator and his assistant. This will require extra camera rehearsals. All these technical challenges will put extra pressure on the actor playing the detective since he will have to do many takes.

One good piece of news is that the director will be able to take advantage of the fact that some of the spoken lines take place off camera. This is true in the opening pull-back move as well as the final move that pushes into the teenager at the end of the scene. Most likely the director would shoot this scene with the actor speaking his lines so that the camera operator would be able to time the "camera performance" to the actor's performance. However, the director would not want to stop the take if the actor muffed a line. This is because the best take of the dialogue can be used with the best camera take and cut together in the edit.

STAGING 7

Here's a variation of the interrogation scene. In this version our view of the scene space is reversed and we are asked to identify closely with the teenager. This is very different from Staging 6 in which we were distanced from the teenager.

As before, the camera performs the same general U-shaped, in-depth movement, but in this case there is no subject that moves along the camera path. Instead, the camera movement is motivated by letting the viewer know that there is important action going on outside the frame. This is accomplished by opening the scene with a closeup of the detective talking to someone (the teenager) who is out of the frame. This strategy is particularly seductive since the detective is almost looking into the camera at us. This kind of direct address reinforces the viewer's understanding that we are not seeing one of the key players in the scene.

This is a far more theatrical staging strategy than the one in Staging 6 forcing us to focus our attention on the detective. In Staging 7 the camera moves slowly through the scene space while the actors are stationary. Not until the end of the shot does the detective come forward to thrust the confession under the teenager's nose.

This entire scene is staged as a continuous master. If done properly, the director could play the whole scene without a single cut.

1

The shot opens with the detective seated in a swivel chair. He is reading a confession for a few moments before looking up in the direction of the camera. The camera begins to dolly back very slowly...

DETECTIVE: This is good reading. Lot's of action.

1a

.. .The camera pulls back until it comes into an extreme OTS shot behind the boy being interrogated...

DETECTIVE: A cop likes this kind of story. But the prosecutor, he's going to love it.

D1

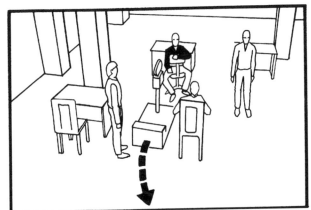

The camera doesn't begin the pull back until the detective starts to speak. The opening of the move is imperceptible.

D1a

The camera stops in the OTS framing and the teenager in the foreground is slightly out of focus due to the limitations of depth of field.

1b

...A second cop leans into the shot and whispers to the boy...

SECOND COP: Detective Fulcro is kinda crazy. You don't want to upset him.

1c

...The second cop exits right and the camera follows him so that it crosses the line. Now we are on an OTS shot on the opposite side of the boy...

DETECTIVE: Kid, haven't you figured out yet that you have no place to hide? This is the end of the line.

D1b

When the cop leans down to speak to the teenager he blocks our view of the detective. This gives the cameraman the chance to rack focus to the foreground.

D1c

The camera rack-focuses during the dolly move right so that the detective is in focus as the camera frames him.

1d

...Detective Fulcro comes forward propelling the wheeled chair forward pushing with his feet. The camera pans down to the confession as Fulcro holds it out to the boy...

DETECTIVE: Just sign this thing, kid, and then we'll be able to help you.

1e

...The camera pans extreme left nearly a half-circle to keep the confession in frame until the boy is in a low angle CU.

D1d

To make the forward dolly move work, the camera has to be out on a short jib arm so the dolly is clear of the teenager's chair as the dolly moves forward. The camera comes in close on the confession. We hold a beat and...

D1e

The camera swings around with the confession until the teenager is framed in CU.

ESTIMATED SCHEDULE

This time let's look at what a real day on the set might include. Our production manager's diary is really a case study covering the typical problems a production might run into.

The crew call is for 8:00 am at the studio. The cast arrives at 8:30 and the rehearsal begins at 9:00. Because of last minute changes in the script, the director decides to add dialogue to the scene. While the actors wait for the new lines, the grips hang lights. The rehearsal goes slowly because the actors are not familiar with the new lines and the director continues to make changes in the rehearsal. By 10:30 the scene is beginning to take shape. The director sees that the actors are losing the edge he is looking for and he decides that more rehearsal will only hurt the performances. The lighting stand-ins come on the set and the DP gets all the lights in place. It is now 10:45. There's a short camera rehearsal with the stand-ins and then the actors are called in. The camera rehearsal with the actors takes about 20 minutes, but it is clear that the final move with the confession is going to be a real challenge.

The director starts to lay down actual takes but the actors miss lines and the director has cue cards made. Finally they get all the way through one take but the operator blows the focus. The director looks at video playback and realizes the final camera choreography just isn't right. They work on adjusting this and practice the new framing. It is now 12:45.

On the next take the soundman hears noise during pre-roll. The soundman hears more noise in the first few seconds of the next take. He begins to check cables until he realizes he's hearing the stomach grumbling of the actor playing the detective. It's just about 1:00 o'clock and they break for lunch.

After lunch they do run through the shot but the producer is still unhappy with the new lines. The director makes some changes and they begin to shoot. It is now 2:30. In the final part of the shot, the actor playing the detective has trouble getting the chair he is on to roll into the right position. Even when he gets it right it looks as though he is struggling.

The decision is made to lower the chair and put it on a western dolly. Grips lying on the floor will guide the dolly and the chair into place. The chair is rigged and the grips practice the move a few times. This system works but is unreliable. At this point, the video tap develops a problem and a cable has to be replaced. After this is corrected, the director begins to lay down some more takes. It is now 3:30. The director shoots 12 takes, make some adjustments and shoots 10 more takes. Including the stuff shot in the morning we are up to take 27.

The writer arrives on the set and listens to one of the takes. It's the first one that works from beginning to end. He tells the director that one of the new lines contains a continuity error. The director, producer, writer, and the script supervisor argue for 15 minutes about whether or not the mistake is significant. They finally decide to change the line. It is 4:30. When they begin shooting, the dolly with the chair on it runs over the foot of the actor as he mimes propelling himself forward. He toughs it out even though his foot is bleeding. He is losing his concentration and the director calls a break.

After the break they begin again and finally get two takes that are usable. At 5:30 the director begins to get coverage. This requires lighting adjustments for each closeup. At 6:30 one of the grips asks which cue card they have been using for the closeups of the detective. Everyone realizes that the actor has been speaking one of the lines that was cut. The director checks the video playback for 15 minutes to find the shot in question and then realizes they stopped recording video right before this shot came up. It is now 7:20. They reshoot the closeups. Wrap is called at 8:35 p.m. It has been a 12-and-a-half-hour day.

While this may sound like a film crew that is seriously confused, it is fairly representative of the type of surprises that happen on the set. This kind of controlled chaos is as typical of great films as the most forgettable ones and if good work is produced, it is because the director and his creative team have remained focused on the vision of the film.

STAGING 8

Here is another dialogue sequence in a moving car. This time we will use a staging style that is a compromise between the long master approach in Staging 3 and the individual closeups that were used in Staging 4. The way to do this is to use a hand-held camera in the car and pan between individual story points. However, it would be visually awkward to do this in a single master, so the scene is divided into shorter shots in which two or three story points are connected by reducing the number of cuts.

Even though the camera is mobile and covers several different angles, most of the action is viewed from a position in the backseat. This does not prevent the director from getting reverse shots by including the rear view mirror in the frame. This becomes a way of showing the person in the back seat without actually doing a reverse shot.

One major choice the director has, is between tripod-steady camera operation or rougher, hand-held documentary-style camera work. The documentary style would make it easier to pan freely within the car. This is because the transition between the subjects in the front and backseat (joined by cuts in the storyboard) could be handled by longer pans than would be permissable if the camera were operated in a more stable style.

In this situation the director is dependent on the camera operator for the "feel" of the shot. Many operators that specialize in hand-held camera work could shoot the car interior and make it look as though it were shot from a tripod. In fact, the director would probably let the operator shoot freely, some of the time, just capturing the action as it happened.

1

We open on a shot of a man driving a car. The driver turns to the man next to him to speak...

DRIVER: What's there to eat?

1a

The camera pans to the passenger sitting next to the driver.

PASSENGER: We're down to a pack of Spearmint.

D1

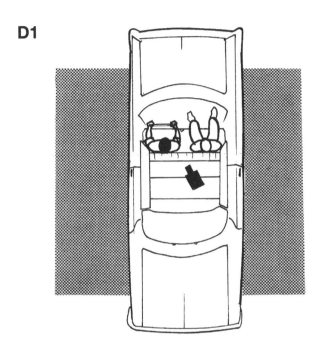

In a confined space, the aspect ratio will affect the shooting style. In the current version the aspect ratio is 1.85: 1. This wide screen format reduces the panning move from the driver to passenger. If we were shooting 1.33:1 the horizontal pan would be more pronounced.

D1a

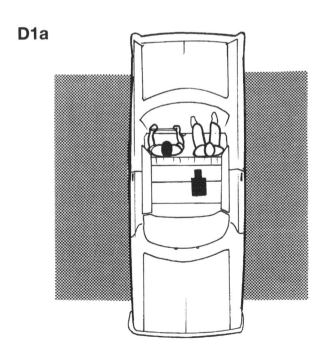

As you can see, cars are clearly visible through the windshield which means that matching shots may become difficult unless the most visible cars are driven by production drivers.

1b

The camera pans with the passenger as he turns and offers gum to a man in the backseat.

PASSENGER: Want a stick of gum?

2

Cut To: A hitchhiker seated on the backseat...

HITCHHIKER: I'll pass ...

D1b

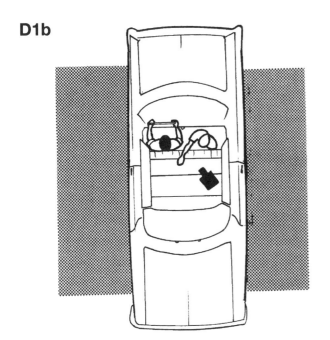

The accompanying story-board shows that we have widened out by zooming back. This reframing will be imperceptible if the zoom happens as the passenger turns around.

Note: characters not included in a shot may be excluded from the diagrams.

D2

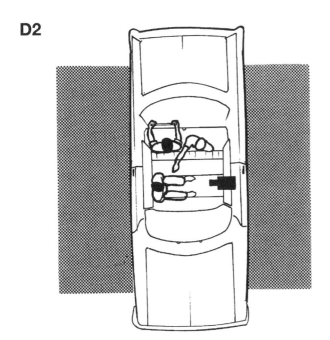

In a wide framing like this, the camera operator might push the camera up against the door and operate the camera from the side. This allows more distance from the subject and a longer focal length lens.

2a

... Pan with the hitchhiker as he sits up and turns to the passenger.

HITCHHIKER: ... I could use a meal more.

3

Cut To: A closeup of the rear view mirror reflecting the face of the hitchhiker...

DRIVER(O.S.): Tollbooth. Who's got change?

D2a

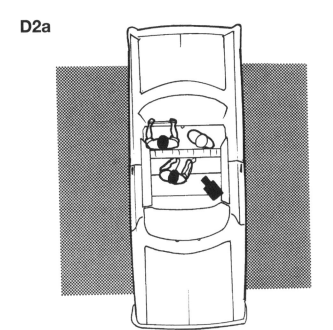

In this and the previous shot the camera is low and tilted up. This means that the only background outside the car that is included in the frame is the sky. Naturally this makes it easier to match backgrounds permitting the production manager greater latitude in selecting roads to shoot on.

D3

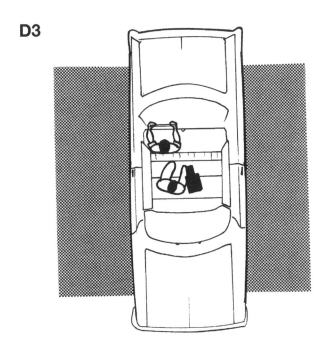

This shot requires the cameraman to shoot in a long focal length which exaggerates camera motion. Most likely, the camerman would brace the camera with a shoulder pod or stand to steady the camera.

3a

Pan down from the mirror a few inches to the road and out the windshield. A police car is only a few cars ahead...

3b

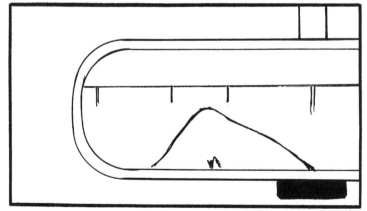

... Pan back up to the rear view mirror. The hitchhiker's face is gone from the mirror. All we see is part of his knee now that he is lying down on the backseat.

D3a

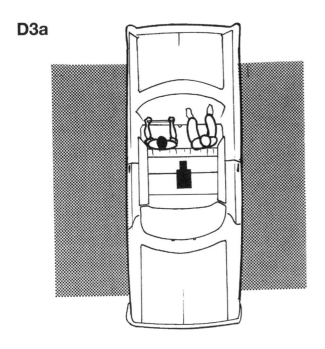

As the camera tilts down, the cameraman shifts focus to the traffic on the highway.

D3b

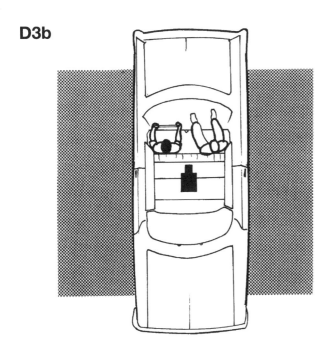

The cameraman tilts back up and shifts the focus back to the mirror.

4

Cut To: The driver looking in the rearview mirror. He looks suspicious because he sees that the hitchhiker is hiding himself...

DRIVER: Tired?

4a

.. .Pan to the backseat.

HITCHHIKER: Yeah, I could use a nap.

D4

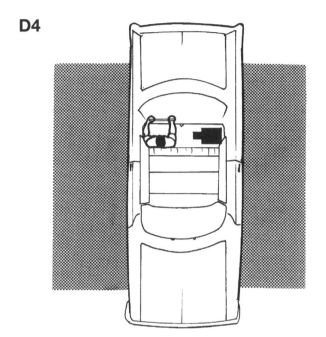

The driver might turn his head or shift his eyes to the mirror as he speaks. This sets up the action for the pan to the backseat in the next panel.

D4a

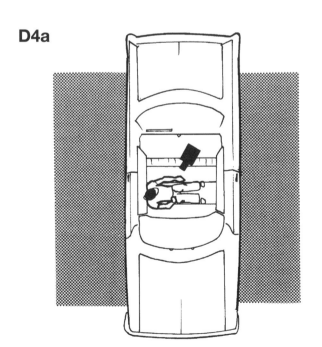

This is a good example of a shot that uses camera movement, however, the closeup of the driver and the medium shot framing of the hitchiker in the backseat can be used separately if necessary. For this to be an option, the director will have to make sure that the camera does not move while either actor is speaking.

TECHNICAL CONSIDERATIONS

Staging 8 is conceived as a low-budget solution. The hand-held camera is a fast way to shoot, and it is even possible to shoot the scene without using a towing car. This, however, is not done without giving something up. Both sound and lighting will suffer if the car is not towed. Naturally, the sound of the car will be audible on the soundtrack since the engine will be running. At the same time, there will be few places to hide the lights, since the camera will be panning around the car with great freedom.

We can shoot Staging 8 using only two camera positions. Because it is easy to make changes when working hand-held, it makes sense to shoot several framings and shot sizes of the key positions. For instance, shots 3, 5 and 6 could easily be recorded with slight changes in shot size by varying the focal length of a zoom lens. By choosing a low-angle position for many of the shots, the sky is included in the background rather than the road. This is helpful because it means that matching the scenery from shot to shot is less of a problem.

As you will have noticed, there is no profile shot of the passenger in the front seat. This is crucial because it means that the entire scene can be shot without having to tow the car. Why? Because the profile shot of the front passenger seat must be taken from the driver's seat. This means towing the car without a driver so that the camera operator can shoot from the driver's side.

ESTIMATED SCHEDULE

8:30 a.m.—Crew call. Two camera cars and two picture cars have been pre-rigged at the end of the previous day. The crew call is later than usual because rush hour must be over in order to get the scene shot on a highway. Since the day will run long, the production manager has scheduled a magic-hour shot for the end of this day.

The actors arrive for makeup at 9:00 a.m. and are ready by 9:45. The director talks over his shot list with the DP and camera operator at this time. Next there is a brief rehearsal with the actors. This scene has been rehearsed before, and the run-through looks good. The director wants to preserve the spontaneity and rehearses for only 20 minutes.

10:15—The picture car and camera car leave the staging area and by 10:30 are moving along the stretch of road chosen for the scene. After the first two takes, a sound problem develops which delays the shooting for 15 minutes. The director uses this time to have the key grip adjust the lighting.

11:00—Shooting resumes and the first series of shots are taken from the front seat position.

12:00—The director postpones lunch to get the shots from the backseat which he thinks he can do quickly. This turns out not to be the case. The first problem is that traffic has begun to pick up during lunch hour and several takes are ruined by truck noise. On several occasions, they come very close to getting an uninterrupted shot before a problem arises.

Clouds have rolled in and the lights have to be readjusted. By 1:30, the last few shots are not completed and the production manager decides it's time to call lunch.

2:30—Shooting resumes. The director is unhappy with the way the scene is playing and changes two lines. This means that one of the shots already checked off the shot list will have to be re-shot so that dialogue continuity is preserved.

The director keeps asking the operator to move the camera to a slightly higher angle on the remaining shots. Now the background is visible and it is obvious that the scenery does not match the scenery surrounding the tollbooth. This is discussed by the production manager, the DP and the director. They decide it will not be a problem and continue to shoot.

3:45—The director is down to the last two shots. Even so, the production is way behind schedule. The final shot is the tollbooth. The production manager is concerned that they will run into rush-hour traffic. The decision is made to shoot the approach to the tollbooth with a wide angle from an overpass and let the dialogue run underneath. This means that the shots looking out from the interior of the car will be eliminated.

All that remains to be done is shot 6, which is a down shot of the backseat. The traffic has increased to the point that road noise is now a problem. The decision is made to fake this shot while the car is parked in a rest area. The car will be rocked to simulate driving motion.

5:30—The final shot of the day is completed.

STAGING 9

In this extended dialogue sequence, extensive repositioning of the actors is combined with camera movement. Unlike the previous strategies in this chapter, which maintained a predominantly frontal orientation, this example allows the camera to view all four sides of the interior at various times in the scene.

Camera movement is also used to move the viewer around the scene and this includes countermoves, reorientation by crossing the line of action and 160 degree pans to make reverses without cuts. Usually this much movement is used only in a scene with considerable dialogue. (Keep in mind that the storyboard has only enough space for a brief suggestion of dialogue.)

One important aspect of Staging 9 is the way that the kitchen table serves as the center point of the action as the characters and the camera change sides throughout the staging. Sometimes the camera follows a character, while other times it moves in the opposite direction of an actor. This means that we are constantly viewing a new part of the location. Normally, this might be disorienting to the viewer. However, the use of camera movement to cross the line and reverse screen direction helps make the geography understandable.

As you read the storyboard, consider how the action determines the movement of the actors and then consider how the arrangement of the action can be invented to force the camera and the actors to move according to a plan.

1

We open on Ann, standing in her kitchen. She approaches the camera...

1a

Her teenage son, Tom, arrives in the doorway holding his hand which is cut...

TOM: Hey, Mom, I got cut—

ANN: Let me see.

D1

Ann walks over to the camera...

D1a

The camera pans around to reframe Ann as she steps into a medium shot. Tom is standing in a doorway and comes forward.

1b

...Ann looks at the cut. It's only a scrape.

1c

...Tom goes around behind the kitchen table. Ann goes to the cabinet to get a BandAid...

D1b

Tom comes forward and joins Ann in a profile
two-shot.

D1c

Ann goes to the right and Tom goes behind the table. The camera begins to
move forward slowly to frame him in a wide, medium shot.

1d

Tom continues to move around the table, counterclockwise. Ann is in the background with her back to the camera...

1e

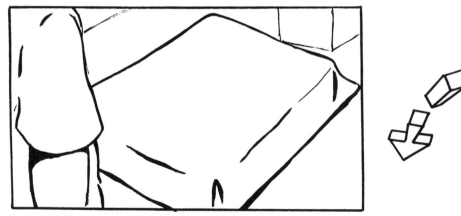

Tom is intrigued by the covered cake pan on the table...

TOM: We having guests or something?

ANN: Stay out of the cake.

D1d

As Tom checks out the food on the table, he is slowly meandering to the left. He comes around to the end of the table and turns in profile to the camera. While this is happening, the camera keeps Tom in frame by dollying left in a quarter-circle, simultaneously moving closer.

D1e

The camera tilts down to the cake pan on the table, continuing the quarterturn counterclockwise. This puts the camera at an angle behind Tom, close to the orientation required for an OTS shot.

1f

The camera tilts down to the cake pan as Tom tries to sneak a look. He lifts up the towel covering the cake and sees some lettering...

2

Cut to: Ann finds the BandAids and closes the cabinet...

D1f

The camera moves forward to the cake pan as Tom reaches down to sneak a peak. We are still in the same continuous dolly shot that opened the scene.

D2

This is a straight locked-off OTS of Ann at the cabinet.

2a

... Ann turns around.

3

Cut to: Tom as he drops the towel covering the cake before he can read the inscription...

D2a

Hold the locked-off shot.

D3

Fast-cut to Tom as he quickly gets his hand away from the cake.

3a

The camera tilts up quickly to Tom who looks as innocent as possible.

4

Cut To: Ann as she comes forward to the camera.

ANN: I hope you didn't cut your hand on that rusty old car in the field.

D3a

The camera makes a fast tilt up from the shot of the cake pan in storyboard 3. (This puts us in a low angle of Tom. Most likely, the director would cover this in other ways, including a version that starts on Tom's face and quickly tilts down to the cake. Another version might be a wider shot of Tom and the cake, all in one frame, without the tilt move.)

D4

Ann turns to the camera and walks to the table. The camera begins pulling back slightly as she approaches...

4a

Ann comes right up to the camera which begins to slowly move back as she comes forward.

ANN: Okay let's see it.

5

Cut to: A close shot of Tom OTS of Ann.

TOM: This better not hurt.

D4a

Ann comes forward, gaining on the backtracking camera until she is in a generous closeup. (To do this, the camera had to backtrack only about four feet.)

D5

The OTS shot comes right after the camera stops moving in storyboard 4a.

6

Cut to: A closeup of Ann OTS of Tom.

ANN: When did you have your last tetanus booster?

7

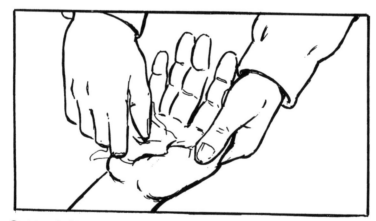

Cut to: A CU of Tom's hand as Ann cleans the scrape.

TOM: OUCH!

D6

Storyboard panels 6–9 are essentially straight OTS coverage shots.

D7

The director would probably shoot additional angles of this shot.

8

Cut To: A closeup of Ann OTS of Tom.

ANN: You're such a faker.

9

Cut to: A closeup of Tom.

TOM: Mom, I need cake to keep my strength up during the recovery period.

SFX: A dog barks.

D8

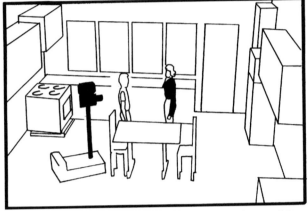

This is the same framing as storyboard panel 6.

D9

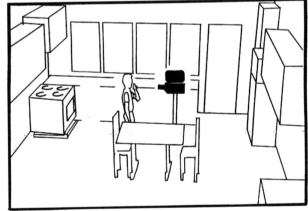

This shot would also be covered as an OTS shot as in storyboard panel 5.

10

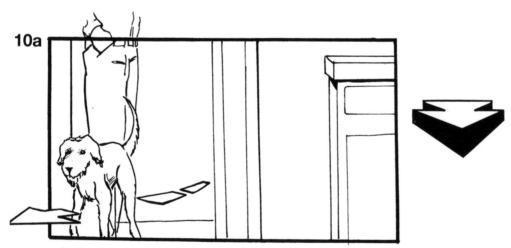

Cut To: A low-angle medium shot of the kitchen door. A dog wants to come inside. Ann crosses the frame as she goes to the door...

10a

... Ann opens the door, and the dog comes in the kitchen. The camera begins to pull back...

ANN: All right, come on in.

D10

The shot starts on the dog and then Ann crosses the frame. The door opens, the dog comes in and then we begin the pullback.

D 10a

Continuing to pullback with the dog. The dog exits the frame, and we tilt up into a medium shot of Ann and continue to widen out.

10b

... Ann turns back to Tom. The camera ends the pullback in a two-shot of Ann and Tom.

TOM: So, when's dinner—and dessert?

ANN: Dinner's in half-an-hour.

10c

.. .Tom turns to the table and Ann crosses behind him to the right. The camera dollies with Ann. Tom pours a glass of milk...
After a moment at rest, the camera begins a countermove to the right as Ann comes forward.

**D
10b**

The pullback move pauses in the two-shot of Ann at the door facing Tom. Up until this point, this move might be only six-to-eight seconds. After the dialogue is spoken Ann begins to walk to the right.

**D
10c**

The camera begins to move again, this time crossing the line as Ann crosses to the right. The camera stops. We pause a moment for dialogue.

10d

After spending a few moments speaking to Tom, Ann comes forward. This is the beginning of a big countermove by the camera.

10e

...Ann passes Tom.

**D
10d**

The camera moves again as Ann comes forward. The camera moves right in a quarterturn, countering move.

**D
10e**

Ann goes right by the camera as the camera passes her in the turning move-ment. The camera tends to favor Tom in this countermove. In other words, the operator might cut off Ann at the top of the frame as she goes by.

10f

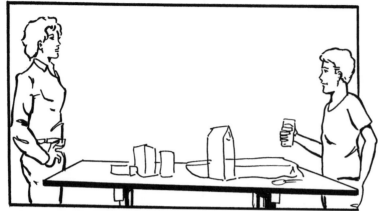

...The countermove ends as Ann reaches the far side of the kitchen table opposite Tom. Now, Tom and Ann are in a profile two-shot.

ANN: Don't go and get filled up on snacks before dinner.

11

Cut to: An angular two-shot of Ann and Tom.

TOM: C'mon Mom, who's the cake for?

D
10f

The entire countermove illustrated in 10d–10f might take 6–8 seconds.

D11

This framing is somewhere between a two-shot and an OTS shot.

11a

... **Ann turns to the camera and begins walking to the cabinet. The camera pans with her...**

TOM: Are you going to tell me or not?

ANN: You obviously don't get the concept of a secret.

11b

.. .**Ann walks right by the camera then she turns around and steps forward into a tighter shot.**

ANN: I can tell you it's not anyone's birthday.

D
11a

The camera backs up slightly, but Ann gains on the camera and passes it.

D
11b

When Ann is just past the camera, she turns back to Tom. The camera has stopped backing up at this point.

12

Cut To: Tom as he comes forward to camera...

12a

.. .The camera pulls back a few feet to include Ann in an OTS shot.

TOM: This is cruel behavior on your part and a very bad example for an adolescent.

D12

Tom approaches Ann, heading toward the camera. The camera pulls back 2–3 feet ahead of him.

D 12a

The pullback move ends in a closeup of Tom OTS of Ann.

SYMPATHETIC MOTION

In Staging 9 we used several camera moves of a type that we have not looked at before. Most camera movement is used to change the size of the shot, emphasize action or move us to a new viewpoint. But there is another type of camera movement that is choreographed around the movement of actors as a way of maintaining a close relationship with a character. We could call this type of camerawork sympathetic motion since it encourages the viewer to identify with the character.

In most cases this type of camera movement covers only a few feet. Since it is synchronized with an actor's movement the camerawork is practically invisible. When moves of this type are used in a scene, they convey a fluid sense of viewpoint and help endorse the physical depth of the scene.

There are several of these moves in Staging 9, in which a character moves forward while the camera backs up. In many cases the character is moving faster than the camera and within two-to-three seconds, the camera stops and the character is framed in a closeup or tight medium shot. Storyboard panels 4–4a and 12–12a are examples of this type of move.

What's the advantage of these shots versus a locked-off camera? Look at storyboard frames 12–12a. First we have to consider that the director wants Tom to start in a wide medium shot and end up in a closeup shot facing Ann. The question is where to place the camera to get this framing. If the director stations the camera at the point at which Tom stops, he gets the closeup, but at this distance, we get a full shot at the opening of the shot and this is too wide. On the other hand, if we place the camera closer to Tom to get the desired medium shot, Tom has to go past the camera to reach Ann.

The only solution to this problem is to dolly the camera to reframe the shot. This allows the director to get the desired framing at the beginning and end of the shot, no matter where the actors are placed in relationship to one another.

TECHNICAL CONSIDERATIONS

Staging 9 is complex by any standards. We might even call it a "studio" staging style since it requires considerable space for the camera moves. It is not the type of work that is attempted without a storyboard or a director accustomed to this controlled type of staging—and there are only a handful that are.

This is also a style that requires precision from the actors. They have to hit their marks and be right on the money or the shot doesn't work. Similarly, the camera operator and dolly grips have to be very exact. This type of camerawork was routine during the studio period of the '30s and '40s when camera operators were practicing these types of camera moves day-in and day-out. This has not been the case for many years.

Staging 9 includes considerable camera movement that follows the actors in medium shots and closeups. Most likely the camera would be put on a dance floor so that it could move fluidly in all directions, crabbing and craning with the action.

One potential problem that might be worth eliminating is the shot of the dog entering the house. By itself, this is not particularly difficult; however, this is just the beginning of a long camera move that combines other elements. It would make sense to plan a very simple version of the action and shoot this first. With a backup version in the can, we can go on to the more difficult moving shot.

Staging 9 contains as much technique as will ever be found in a dialogue sequence. Properly handled, this type of staging is very effective, and, contrary to popular wisdom, it can be less stagy-looking than other, less-complex camera setups.

SCHEDULING AND COVERAGE

How long will this scene take to shoot? All day and then some. If we shoot on location, figure half-again as much time. Fortunately, this is a light, humorous scene. It would not be unreasonable to assume that the actors would be able to be fairly consistent. If the dramatic requirements were more demanding, the entire process could get bogged down very quickly.

This raises the issue of coverage and stylistic consistency. In the stagings we have looked at so far, coverage was always available as an alternative to a long, continuous master shot. However, coverage is not as easily integrated into Staging 9. This is because the dolly moves are necessary to follow the considerable movement of the actors. If the dolly moves are cut, it becomes necessary to simplify the choreography of the actors as well.

This means that the director has to be fairly confident that he can bring this scene off from beginning to end.

INTERVIEW HAROLD MICHELSON

Harold Michelson has been a motion picture Art Director, Production Illustrator and Visual Consultant for more than 30 years. His long list of credits includes *The Birds, The Graduate, Catch 22, Terms of Endearment, History of the World Part One, Dick Tracy* and *Hoffa.*

Would you describe how visualization and staging methods have changed over the last 40 years?

The old Art Departments used to create illusions of ordinary things all the time. They built or painted in ceilings, walls or whole parts of the set. Today, this is done by special effects companies and a lot of the Art Directors don't know how to do things like forced perspective. These have become techniques that are used largely for fantasy films.

Because most films are shot on location?

Yes. A lot of directors stage things like a play. They want the whole environment, but then they find out that they cannot always get the shots they want. There are lots of restrictions on location.

In Terms of Endearment, *for example, I was the Art Director. Tom Wright was the storyboard artist, and he laid out the shots for a location that was a real house. He showed actors coming in right to left in a bedroom and going over to a*

crib to see a baby. Well, the sketch showed a full figure, but the room was too small to get the camera back. In order to get the shot, we had to build a tower outside the house and shoot through the window. We backed up ten feet from the window and this gave us the additional distance needed to get the full shot. This is a lot of extra work for a shot that would be simple on a sound stage.

But isn't it true that on a sound stage you don't always build the whole set, so there are restrictions there as well?

That's right, but when you build partial sets you know what you are going for. You build what you need based on a plan.

A staging plan, presumably worked out in a storyboard?

A storyboard based on a set. When shooting in the studio was the norm, the storyboard was used to show the director how he could use the set.

But the director could describe anything and you could give it to him?

Anything within the budget. Sets are much more economical if you build only what the camera can see. That's the point. The camera has a very limited view. With cutting, and the use of foreground elements to hide the background, the camera may actually include very little of a set.

Because a movie set can be based on illusion?

Yes. For instance, what does it take to show a nightclub in a movie? You start on the handle of the door and the door opens, but it takes up two-thirds of the screen. Down in a corner you have a little L set and two people in a booth and you cut into them. In the meantime, there's smoke in the foreground and a waiter goes by and you get the feeling this is a big nightclub. Well, this is the way movies were done for a long time. Today, you go on location and you get the whole interior. But when it gets down to it, you can't get a wide shot because there is not enough room to get the camera back.

When you are describing the handle of the nightclub door, you are get-

ting into the area of all the shorthand devices that we tend to call cinematic.

Exactly. A lot of the things that are interesting, storytelling images, are things that came about to compress time so that a set didn't have to be built completely. Something small can stand for something big and as it turns out, this is often much better storytelling.

But even in a controlled studio environment, you can't do that unless you plan it out.

Right. But a lot of times today, the director will have a complete set built because he hasn't made up his mind about the staging. He wants the whole environment there so he can think about it.

This brings up the issue of budget and time. How many productions are there that can tie up a stage with a full set, so the director can visit it while he works out his staging?

Not many. Remember the budget is a pretty powerful thing and you want to put your money in the stuff that really counts. You try to find out from the director what he will need and what he expects to see. You kind of know what things can be built within the budget and what can't. So you give the director some sketches of the set and ask, "Are you contemplating low shots?" If he is, you know you have to put in the ceiling.

Some directors believe that sets don't feel like the real thing. There are even those who don't like wild walls.

It doesn't have to be stagy. And you can mix real locations with studio sets. This was the way we worked on The Graduate. *The houses we picked were real houses, but the interiors were completely built on a stage. We replicated real interiors. For backings, we used a real house with a swimming pool. We'd go from Beverly Hills back to the stage. The production designer, Dick Sylbert, designed the sets. I would try to get the action worked out with storyboards and when it all went together, it was seamless.*

In *The Graduate*, were partial sets created to save money by creating the illusion of space?

We didn't have to, because we were creating only small interiors, not a palace or museum.

This raises an interesting paradox. Because of the space limitations of a real location, you may have to

resort to editing or to camera techniques that don't preserve spatial continuity, while a studio set may permit you to use the moving camera and longer master shots that are associated with more realistic techniques. In the final analysis, a studio set may in some ways be more "realistic."**

Just because you are creating parts of a set on a sound stage doesn't mean that you shoot the set only in pieces. If you know that you are going to do a tracking shot in a set, you can create the necessary backgrounds so that you can move continuously.

We had a long continuous shot in The Graduate *where Benjamin comes down the stairs and we follow him through the party. So we created the set we needed for the shot and let the camera roam. But the idea for the shot came first.*

Was this worked out in a storyboard?

Yes. It was all projected.

You mean camera angle projection?

Yes. I'd take the plan for the set and create storyboards that showed what the camera would see with a lens of a specific focal length.

Do you give the director the same shot framing comparing different lenses?

Sure. You try different things. There's give and take with the director as you work out the action.

You use camera angle projection to plot your storyboards and you specify the lens. How do cinematographers react to this?

If possible, I ask the cameraman during preproduction what lenses he likes to use. If he has strong preferences, then I'll project for lenses of that focal length. But the reason I project is that it's the only way to find out if a certain shot is going to work. For instance, if you are shooting on a location and the director wants to shoot out the front door from a camera position at the top of a stairs, you won't know whether you will see the actor coming up the walkway unless you project. That's why I take measurements on location and project the shots that are in some way restricted.

Do you create more than one draft of the storyboard?

Absolutely. I get a lot of rejects. The director may reject an idea or I may decide something isn't working or we

may both decide there's a better solution.

Right now, I'm doing a movie with a scene that is set on a train, where a man is shot. I worked out the second part where the girl shoots the guy and then I went back to the beginning of the scene. You don't necessarily work in continuity. Once I knew what the final shot looked like, I could go back from there and lead up to it.

Some directors really like working with a scene as it evolves on paper. Your choices are unbelievable when you're drawing. Now, think of the same choices when the director is standing on the set the day of the shoot, with 50 people standing around waiting. I mean, to me, it doesn't make any sense not to have a plan before you go in.

What's your first step when you start a new film?

Well, I have to begin with the director and hear what he's thinking about each scene. It may be that he wants his characters to be placed at different heights, so that one of them is looking way down at the other. And then I begin to draw. After all, it's only paper. Things can be changed. But you have to start some-

where. When I work, I have the script right in front of me. The script is the thing.

Do you go to rehearsals?

On The Graduate, *I went to rehearsals. The floor was marked off based on the set that would be built and I walked around on the rehearsal stage. I maneuvered around on the stage with my pad and made little sketches, not to show anybody, but for myself, as reference. I used these to work up ideas at my drafting board. But this was an exception. I don't usually go to rehearsals.*

Are there certain staging techniques or styles that you prefer or others you don't like?

There are directors who follow rules or have signatures. And when you work for someone like that you go along with it. I have never arrived at those kind of rules

for myself, because that's not my job. I don't know what I am going to do until I get there and see the script. I base my decisions on what is right for the story.

Your storyboards are very graphic because of the way you use very expressive blacks and tone. You always seem to be dividing the frame with dark and light areas that determine the staging.

It's funny, some directors don't want to see the shading. But that's part of what I do. I don't draw diagrams. If a director wants diagrams he can hire a football coach.

Shading helps me shape the action. If I cut two-thirds of the screen with black and there's a strip of white light on the side, I've done it for a reason. It's not just decorative. It's there to push the eye.

6 STAGING IN LARGE SPACES

Staging in large spaces is more than just a matter of shooting wide shots or following the subject over a long distance. Presumably, the choice of any setting is based on the practical necessities of the story—to establish the mood, atmosphere or symbolic content of a scene. In this sense, size and space are frequently a matter of emphasizing the emotional distances between characters or between a character and the audience. Stanley Kubrick is a master at using open space to frame the drama. He often set his scenes in cavernous sets as a way of diminishing the power of his characters to control events.

Wide shots and extended dolly shots are useful techniques for exploiting space; however, staging action in large spaces is also an exercise in scale. For scale to be effective, shots of varying size must be contrasted. Therefore, staging action in a large space has a lot to do with moving from near to far shots, or vice versa. And this change of scale can be repeated throughout a scene.

One way to map out choreography in a large space is by looking at a floor plan of the set or location. This non-camera view may help you discover new ways of thinking about how a scene might be staged. Also, it will force you to consider some of the technical aspects of lighting, camera movement and scheduling. Why does examining a plan-view force these issues to the surface? Because, it allows you to simultaneously see the space the camera will view, plus the space needed for dolly track, the crew and the lighting equipment.

Stagings 10 and 11 are based on the floor plan on the following page. What we are looking at, are two rooms connected by a wide opening. At the far ends of each room are doorways, while both rooms are lit by very large picture-windows along the right-hand wall.

The scene involves three people: a middle-aged brother and sister who arrive in the room first, and their father who arrives later. The brother and sister have come to the house where they grew up, which is now for sale. There is no furniture and the rooms are empty. The brother and sister discuss their failure to stay in touch over the years.

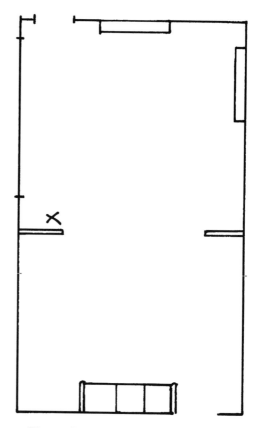

Floor plan for Stagings 10 and 11.

STAGING 10

This is a relatively simple staging in which we split the scene space into two halves and use a pair of reverse setups to view the action. The feeling of large, open space is emphasized by full shots used to frame the characters in the majority of shots. This is a somewhat atypical treatment of the drama when you consider that the subject of the scene is one character's reminiscence of an unhappy childhood. Normally, we would expect to use closeups to see the character's expressions and to give a sense of intimacy to the scene.

The theme of the drama is the remoteness of the characters who have difficulty connecting emotionally. They remain at the edges of the room and never go to the center, keeping the entire room between them. Even the camera is not permitted to approach the characters too closely. The only time the camera comes close to the subjects is in the opening shot. This is used as contrast to the shots that follow.

After the opening dolly move, the camera movement is largely a matter of panning with the subject. The pan is very much under-used today, a shame, because it is a very useful technique that also happens to be easy to execute. Another recent trend is choosing shot size based on whether a movie will be released for television or for the theater. The current wisdom, which in my opinion is overstated, is that television is a closeup medium and that long shots do not have sufficient impact on the smaller screen. This does not take into consideration that withholding information discreetly is as much a part of drama as making every moment clear.

1

We open with a wide shot of Eric and Linda, a brother and sister. Eric approaches from the far side of the room. The camera dollies toward him and Linda...

1a

...The camera moves into a medium two-shot and stops. Eric pauses to speak to Linda for a moment. He then walks in front of her and exits the frame on the right...

ERIC: The place looks deserted.

D1

Note: When a figure has a black shirt or a jacket, it means they are included in the camera frame. When the shirt or jacket becomes white, the subject is positioned off-camera.

The camera move is timed to end when Eric reaches Linda.

D1a

The camera favors Linda so that as Eric passes by, the camera reframes slightly to keep her centered.

1b

Linda slides down the wall staring straight ahead. She pays no attention to Eric. When she has been seated for just a moment, she gives Eric the slightest look motivating the cut...

2

Cut to: Eric staring out the window. The camera holds on him for several seconds before he speaks...

ERIC: I used to pretend this window was on the bridge of a ship.

D1b

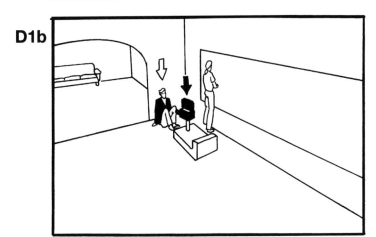

Linda sits down and the camera cranes down with her while dollying in closer.

D2

We begin a long pullback move.

2a

Eric begins to turn and slowly walks along the window, speaking as he goes.

ERIC: The lawn doesn't really look like the ocean, so I pretended the ship was grounded.

2b

...Eric continues forward very slowly as he talks about the past.

ERIC: I guess I was pretty literal-minded even when I was imagining stuff.

D2a

Typically the camera starts a pullback turning move of this type just a moment before the actor begins to move.

D2b

The camera continues to pull back and away from Eric, panning to keep him in the frame.

2c

Eric walks all the way to the far side of the room and reaches up to stretch himself, grabbing on to the top of the door frame.

ERIC: Did dad say he was going to come?

3

Cut to: Linda. This is a dead-on shot.

LINDA: He doesn't talk to me, remember?

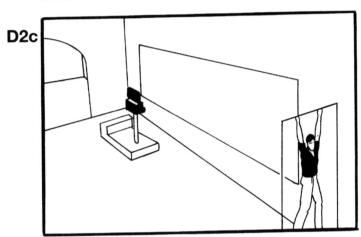

D2c

The dolly move stops just before Eric reaches the door. This is done because a cut works better on a static frame.

D3

This shot would probably be shot from the same low angle position used for storyboard panel 1b. This emphasizes Linda's unchanging, unaffected presence.

4

Cut to: An extreme wide shot. Linda is very small in the frame...

4a

...Eric enters the shot.

ERIC: He doesn't talk to me much either—maybe that's something to be grateful for. Our talks were never all that great.

D4

This leap backward in the scene space produces a cut that might be too extreme for the deliberate pace of the drama. The alternative is to remove shot 3.

D4a

Eric's entrance into the frame could be staged many ways. He could enter very close to the camera or in a very generous medium shot as shown here.

4b

The camera pans slightly with Eric. We hear a door open and close and then hear footsteps on the stairs. Eric's father comes into the room.

ERIC: Being back here and hearing him coming, I feel like I've done something wrong. You know, like I'm about to get grounded.

4c

Eric turns back and sees his father standing in the room.

ERIC: Hey, Dad.

D4b

Eric comes closer to the camera. Again the framing is remote, but it is a simple change to bring him right up to the camera, if the director wants to see Eric's expressions more clearly.

D4c

Eric's father arrives before he turns around. The viewer sees Eric's father's entrance before Eric.

5

Cut To: Eric and Linda's father in low-angle medium shot. After he speaks to Eric he comes forward...

FATHER: Eric. You forgot to close the door behind you on your way in.

5a

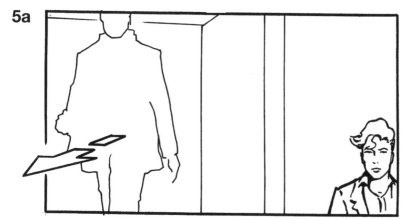

... As Eric's father comes forward, the camera tilts down and pans to Linda swinging left in a semicircle.

D5

This is a relatively low-angle shot. This additional angle change helps smooth the cut from the previous shot and sets up the upcoming camera move.

D5a

There are several ways to choreograph this action. Overall, the choices depend on the order in which things happen. Does the father leave the frame before we pan to Linda or do we begin the pan before the father moves?

5b

Cut to: a medium shot of Linda watching Eric and her Father greet each other.

6

Cut To: A reverse low-angle of Eric and his father.

D5b

Most likely the shot would have Linda look away right after the camera move stops, so that the cut is made on her head turn.

D6

This shot could be framed many ways and falls into the category of coverage. In this version, the camera frames Linda's general point-of-view.

CAMERA STYLE

Staging 10 is conceived in a more modern style than some of the other stagings we have looked at so far. While still well within the bounds of the continuity style, the wide and open staging leaves room for more formal and graphic framings and cutting patterns. Some of this might be emphasized by making cuts that are not on the action, as is generally the rule in classic editing practice. The cutting pattern in panels 2c — 3 — 4 is a good example of a potentially jarring cut. The juxtaposition of frames 3 and 4 really emphasizes distance and space and is a highly commentative cut. At the same time, Eric's entrance into the open frame is not an invisible way to make the transition between shots 3 and 4. All these choices disrupt our emotional connection with the characters.

Finally, there is the lens choice and framing to consider. Storyboard panel 4 gives Eric considerable head room. This type of center framing emphasizes the space rather than the subject and prevents him from completely dominating the shot. Most of the other framings in this scene are relatively traditional, but with only a few adjustments, such as centering the subject in the frame and adding head room, the viewer's relationship to the characters can be easily distanced.

Wide lenses were used for most of these shots which are in the 24–30mm range. Since the room is 25 × 22 feet, this allows us to get wide compositions without excessive bending of vertical lines, particularly since there are no foreground elements used as framing devices.

A CASE STUDY

If Staging 10 was roughed out in an on-set rehearsal, the actors and director would walk through the scene in the morning. The director and cinematographer make the decision that the windows should be the primary source of light. This means that the cinematographer would be faced with a wide range of lighting values all in one shot.

Let's suppose the director decides to make changes in the staging on set. The following conversation might take place between the director and the cinematographer:

Director: Don't like the cut to Eric at the window. In fact I'd like to make the whole scene one shot.

DP: So, how do we get from Linda to Eric—or don't we stay with her now?

Director: We stay with Linda when she sits down but then we pull back and pan over to Eric.

DP: But we just craned down to her. We'll be panning over to Eric in an extreme low angle.

Director: I don't like that.

DP: What if we pan over to his feet?.

Director: Yeah, he's talking about the window. Maybe he plays with his shadow on the floor and we're looking at the shadows.

DP: We have the technology.

Director: Then we pan around with him and follow him all the way down to the other side of the room....You're shaking your head?.

DP: This is a lot of camera movement for a monologue.

Director: We have to get to the other side of the room so we can look back at Linda.

DP: What if we just stay on one side of the room near where Eric makes the turn at the window and let him go wherever he wants in a long shot. Just forget the reverse.

Director: That solves some problems.

DP: Lots of problems. You can always cut to Linda.

Director: And we can pull back to Eric's father.

DP: You mean at the end of the shot? That's possible. In fact that might work out really well.

Director: You know, it will probably be stronger without Linda.

DP: Keep telling yourself that.

Director: Let's try a rehearsal.

STAGING 11

Our next staging takes the remoteness of the characters in Staging 10 one step farther. This time we will preserve frontality and eliminate the reverse shots used previously. Since we are not going to cut to a reverse shot, we can hold Eric in a long unbroken take.

But this is the only major change we will make, and the staging of the characters is essentially the same.

Compare this approach with the previous staging in which we cut to a reverse angle for the second half of the scene. A third major approach to scene space was shown in Staging 9 in which the camera circles around action centered at the kitchen table.

Taken together, Stagings 9, 10 and 11 represent the three basic approaches to scene space for all scenes:

1) The camera is outside the action looking inward from a single direction.

2) The camera is in the action looking outward.

3) The camera is outside the action but combines views from opposing directions.

The 3 stagings are also numbered in the order of technical difficulty beginning with the simplest approach. In this case, difficulty refers to the amount of space that has to be lit, decorated and propped as well as the consequent movement of equipment around the set.

STAGING 11

1

We open in a full two-shot of Eric and Linda. Eric enters the room in the background and heads for the wide opening between the two rooms. The camera dollies in slowly.

1a

The camera continues in slowly...

ERIC: The place looks deserted.

D1

The shot would probably begin with Linda in the shot and have Eric enter the frame in the background.

D1a

The camera move forward would be timed to end in the medium two-shot in storyboard panel 1b.

1b

...The camera moves in on Linda, as Eric exits the frame on the right side...

1c

...The camera cranes down and pulls back as Linda takes a seat on the floor...

D1b

We hold this position while they speak for a moment.

D1c

Eric's crossing wipes the frame and this helps hide the beginning of the camera move down and back. The camera stops in a low-angle, full shot of Linda seated.

1d

...The camera pans left to Eric's shoes. He's stepping in and out of the window light that falls on the floor. He plays with his shadows...

ERIC: Remember doing this, Linda? The sunlight was the best part of this room.

1e

...The camera makes a big circular turn following Eric as he walks away from Linda...

ERIC: Isn't this where the wall tapestry was?

LINDA: Yeah, the fake oriental thing.

D1d

It might be necessary to hide an additional dolly backward while the pan moves to Eric's feet.

The camera begins a quarter-turn to the left. This begins the big shift of viewpoint to the opposite side of the set.

D1e

The camera continues the quarter-turn while panning with Eric.

1f

...The camera continues to pan with Eric. He pauses frequently while walking, to soak up the look of the room and all the memories it brings back...

ERIC: This'll be the first time I've seen Dad in three years.

1g

...The camera dollies right as it pans with Eric. The camera stops with Eric as he pauses in the corner...

ERIC'S FATHER (O.S.): You left the front door unlocked Eric. Not real smart.

D1f

The camera continues the pan, as Eric saunters around the room. It is a matter of taste whether the camera continues to dolly when Eric pauses during his walk. Some directors think it calls attention to the camera if the shot continues to move when the subject stops walking in the middle of a shot.

D1g

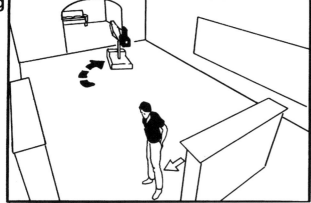

We dolly across the set but let Eric move faster than the camera so that, when the camera stops, the camera ends up in the middle of the room.

1h

...The camera pulls back (from the broken line medium-shot framing) to reveal Eric's father standing at the edge of the room. Eric turns around to face him.

2

Cut to: Linda. She is not even looking in the direction of her father.

D1h

Note: We are viewing the room from the reverse side for this diagram.

This pullback move is cued by Eric's father's off-screen line. Compare this with the reveal of the father in Staging 10.

D2

This is our first cut in the entire sequence. Since we can now expect the scene to continue with exchanges of dialogue instead of a virtual monologue, shorter shots and faster cutting might be more appropriate.

TECHNICAL CONSIDERATIONS

This type of staging requires that the entire action be worked out carefully in rehearsal. The camera movement is ambitious, particularly the shift from Linda sitting down, to the closeup of Eric's feet.

The camera moves shown in the storyboard could be obtained with the Steadicam or Panaglide system or a dolly. However, the scene space in Staging 10/11 is open, and it would be easy to lay down dance floor. This means that a good dolly crew could work quickly, and contrary to what many filmmakers believe, the overall time saved by using a Steadicam could be slight. There is also the question of the "feel"of the moving shot. Because Eric's walk around the room is slow, the motion of the Steadicam would be more noticeable.

COVERAGE

A director could take more chances with this scene since he can expect to cover 1-2 pages of script with only a few setups. Also, the location is an open space and this makes all the production requirements, from props to lighting, easier to deal with.

On a theatrical feature, a director would have time to spend a day shooting this scene and this would include simplified coverage. The director would probably pick up extra shots of Linda reacting to Eric's speech. It would also make sense to shoot a simplified version of the dolly shot in which Linda sits down and the camera pans to Eric's feet. This would be done as a wide master without the dolly move.

INTERVIEW VAN LING

Van Ling was the Creative Supervisor and Visual Effects Coordinator for director James Cameron on *The Abyss* and *Terminator 2*. He is the Director of Creative and Technical Affairs for Lightstorm Entertainment and is on the advisory board of the American Film Institute-Apple Computer Center for Film and Videomakers.

Would you explain the difference between the staging of an action sequence and an effects sequence?

What effects sequences and action sequences have in common is the expense and unrepeatability of such things as stunts, explosions and other gags. What differs is that in the former, these gags often take place removed from the principal action, such as a miniature or bluescreen stage, while in the latter they take place live on the location.

Since the editing is usually very quick and dynamic in an action sequence, the primary emphasis in shooting is the intelligible staging and coverage of the elements. When you have edits as short as three frames long, it is vital to make the geography of the action very clear to the audience so that it's not confusing. You establish the screen direction and stick to it and get lots of coverage.

In a sequence involving effects shots, it is imperative to plan out your staging

because oftentimes you can only choose one specific camera angle or move for a particular effects shot. Because of the cost of doing effects shots, particularly optical or digital composites, you normally can't shoot them like regular production footage and then have the effects house just 'add the effect.' With the new digital and motion control technologies it is becoming easier to loosen up the camera, but it is still fairly expensive, so you have to choose the most effective places in a sequence to use effects shots and that means you have to plan out the sequence carefully in order to maximize the effect. Effects scenes often involve intercutting footage shot miles and months apart and having them match seamlessly, so the planning is crucial.

How would you describe the visualization process from initial concept to the final execution?

When writing the script we tend to visualize certain things fairly specifically. We might do location scouting while we are working on the script. For example, on the canal chase in Terminator 2, *Jim and Bill Wisher, the two co-writers, went to look at the flood control channels to take into account the general look of the place when they were writing the chase.*

Later, when we were farther along in production, Jim went back to the locations and shot video tape. At the same time, the Art Department went to the canal sites and took a lot of measurements.

Around this time, the storyboarders were working with Jim to sketch out the sequence. The information in the storyboard makes the action very specific. We begin to get an idea of what kind of rigging, camera car, and lighting, etc. we will need. We know on what side of the location we will stage equipment for a shot and what elements have to be cleared or dressed in the background.

Do you get the whole production team together to look at the storyboards?

Yes, there are a few big, team meetings with the creative team throughout preproduction.

Who would be at the meetings?

Jim Cameron, the producers, the storyboard artist and the effects or stunt artists involved in the sequence being discussed. We would all be sitting around a scale model with the storyboards, working out the details of the scene. We might use a miniature camera live in the model and act out the action at the meeting. Everyone would be watching the monitor. With this kind of visualization we could preview shots as they were suggested in the meeting. Models are a big help because even storyboards can be interpreted different ways.

When you begin shooting, how closely do you stick to the storyboards?

We usually end up storyboarding a wish list. What Jim always does is go to the location with his director's finder and we take our video camera, and we take a lot of measurements. Now, in the canal chase in T2 we shot in several locations, each site selected for some visual element, but we had to put it all together so it looked like a single connected location on the screen. Often we had to match one part of the canal where the walls were narrow to a loca-

tion where the walls were farther apart or where one side was sloped while in another location the walls were straight. The storyboards gave us a basis of action so we knew exactly what had to happen and kept us from losing sight of the flow of action while contending with all the matching and continuity concerns on location.

One thing I've really noticed with action scenes is that even with storyboards we should have coverage from both sides of the line when it's easy to obtain. It will never cut exactly the way we think it will cut. If we don't have overlap and other things we can use, we are in serious trouble.

There are effects shots and then shots that have effects in them. In an effects sequence, we stuck to the storyboards very closely, because often everything needed to be created from scratch. A model is often built to be seen only from one side, based on the storyboard. The placement of a hidden support wire or pylon is determined by the camera angle in the storyboard, so every little change could have big cost and time ramifications.

You scan some of your storyboards into the computer. Why?

One reason is that we use the computer as a glorified Xerox machine. This is because the computer makes better copies of half-tone artwork. But the main advantage of scanning the storyboards into a digital format is that we can do image-processing with software programs like Adobe PhotoShop.

What kind of image processing are we talking about?

Well, Jim might look at an image and say this would work better if it were flipped. So, instead of having an artist redraw the panel, I would flip it in the computer. I could also remove a figure from the background or foreground or make changes in the framing. This saves the artists a lot of time.

What other new tools do you use?

We have been using the Toshiba IK-M30A. It's a miniature camera about the size of your thumb. It can focus from 5mm to infinity. What you do with it is build study models of your sets and shoot video. That's how we visualized the steel mill sequence at the end of T2. The Art Department went to a defunct steel mill and measured the hell out of it. Then they built a scale model on a five-foot by five-foot table. We were then able to put the miniature camera in the model and move it around to get angles. Jim was really able to assess the need for camera cranes and rigging for a scene. Similarly, the Art Department was able to augment the model of what was actually in the steel mill with models of the sets they were going to build at the location.

You mean things like staircases that originally didn't exist on site?

Right. For example, the art department designed a conveyor belt with a big gear drive for the steel mill scene. They built a miniature of this new set piece for our table top steel mill. Jim could move the set piece around and preview shots using the Toshiba camera.

Even on the actual location a lot of the set pieces were "wild" [pieces of the set that can be moved in and out of position] so that we could move them around to line up the best composition.

Do you mean that you had prop machines, girders, pipes and walls that you could arrange in the shot

so that you could get better compositions?

Yes. Cheating these types of things is standard procedure, but not so much to get better composition as just to get a decent composition at all. If you're shooting in a narrow corridor of machinery walls for example, it's nearly impossible to get a good lateral angle unless you use a very distorting wide angle lens or you have the ability to move the walls a bit. The steel mill was treated more like a set than a location, since most of the foreground and featured set pieces were fabrications anyway. But you only cheat the set arrangement enough to get a composition that helps you tell your story, since you do have to maintain a degree of continuity in the geography.

But all this stuff was previewed using the miniature camera with a scale model and little action figures. We also used this with a video printer that prints on thermal paper like a fax machine. We were able to create storyboard panels or at the very least, blueprints that the storyboard artists used as a guide for fully shaded drawings.

Did you ever try to cut together the video footage into a sequence?

We did more videomatics [a rough edited sequence using storyboard panels or other visualization footage] for The Abyss. *We used that a lot with the submarine models. We would take the models and move them by hand like puppeteers or we might use a cardboard box to represent the corner of a building. This may look funny but it is a really effective way to represent the ballistics and basic dynamics of a shot, and we can do them really quickly.*

In some cases, when we were editing effects scenes with the actual completed shots, we would shoot film of the video monitor while we moved the sub models around by hand. Then we would cut the film footage into an in-progress effects sequence. Even the crude videomatic footage presented a better representation of the dynamics of a shot than a storyboard panel or a slug [black footage inserted in place of a shot that is not available].

Do you use video to previsualize full-scale staging?

Yes, but usually only for effects or action shots. We might use a camcorder to set

up shots of the characters that were being combined with effects. If necessary, we grab someone out of the hallway at the production offices to shoot them for a few minutes.*

Let's talk about the staging on the set. How often do you use multiple cameras?

Apart from action sequences, where we might have as many as eleven cameras, we might use two or three cameras for dramatic scenes. This way we get a closeup and medium shot simultaneously. Another multiple camera situation might have the A camera shooting a profile tracking shot of two actors walking. The B camera could be placed at a right angle so that the actors are approaching the camera. It is usually more cost effective to save time by shooting with multiple cameras than eliminating the cost of the additional operator and camera

Or with ensemble scenes you can get your master of two or three people and then have other cameras with longer lenses picking up closeups so we get our coverage in half as many takes.

How often do you use extended master shots?

Well, a good example was the first Cyberdyne lab early in T2 when we first meet Dyson. The lab was built on a sound stage and was made up of large rooms that were all connected. It made sense in a set like this to move through it without cutting; in other words, to show the reality of it by showing the totality of it.

There was a lot of activity with people working in the scene and also a lot of equipment such as computer screens that had to be working. It took us quite a while to get this up and running. Therefore, if it was going to take us three hours to get the master, it made sense to use the master for the whole sequence. If we didn't do this, then it would still take us three hours to shoot the master and coverage would require an additional two hours. Shooting it all at once just meant rehearsing a little more carefully.

The decision was used to shoot this with Steadicam. It tends to give the shot a slightly edgy, documentary feeling which is what Jim wanted. In the hands of a Steadicam operator like Jimmy Muro, who did the Steadicam work on T2, we get what amounts to a camera performance. I think it took us seven takes to do the scene.

Now, how did the staging of this scene evolve?

In the previous scene, we end on a shot of a television screen in the mental hospital. The decision was made to start the next scene on a monitor in Cyberdyne showing a computer graphic of the prototype chip based on the remains of the Terminator in the original movie. We pan from the monitor and rack focus to the real chip on the table. And then we pan to Dyson and a computer scientist in the background looking at another computer monitor.

Jim knew these were the storytelling elements he wanted to show, but the actual placement of the camera and the choreography is created and refined in rehearsal on the set. We adjust the position of props, furniture and actors to get the framing we want at every stage in the shot. And of course we're moving extras through the frame, in this case, Cyberdyne employees. Jim would adjust the positions and timings of exits and entrances while watching the scene on a video tap or on a Watchman.

How much rehearsal with the actors is there prior to shooting?

Jim usually has a week or two of script read-throughs with the actors prior to the start of principal photography. But this is for working out the performance and the character arc and the emotion rather than the blocking. Jim does this completely divorced from the set.

Then, on the day of the shoot, the actors are in character and these characters are responding to the reality of the location or the set. Jim will work out the blocking at this time allowing the actors to move. As it begins to take shape, he might say to an actor, "Okay if you are going to stop walking over there, then I can put my camera here and you will walk right into a closeup."

How much time is spent blocking a reasonably complex scene?

Every scene is different, but one-and-a-half to two hours is reasonably representative. Then we might spend another hour lighting the set using stand-ins while the actors are getting prepared in costume and makeup. When the actors return to the set, we fine-tune the lighting and the blocking. This might take 30 minutes. After this we're ready to shoot.

What about moving shots?

Moving shots are the most dynamic, but they have to help tell the story and not just be used for the sake of being dynamic, or it becomes very conscious to the viewer. They have to have a purpose, ideally a beginning and ending like a little story in itself.

One of the bad things about moving shots is that if we are not careful, we cannot cut in and out of them. I've noticed that Jim designs his long moving shots so that they have multiple uses. What I mean is that it's possible to use them as a continuous shot or as individual shots. He does this by making sure his long master shots include different compositions, such as closeups and changes of angle within the move. And all these changes are clearly separated and held as if they are locked-off shots.

7 STAGING FOR MULTIPLE SUBJECTS

When four or more characters have significant roles in a scene, coverage can become quite cumbersome. Unless the scene is shot in very long takes, obtaining medium shots and close-ups for each subject can amount to dozens of shots. As the number of players increases, so does the need for a clear shooting plan.

The most obvious way to shoot scenes with several subjects is to shoot the characters in groups. Seated groupings are fairly straightforward since the positioning of the players is fixed and the viewer is easily oriented. But when several characters are standing and moving within the scene space, the director is faced with the challenge of presenting a visually coherent scene.

A director may start blocking the scene with a character-by-character approach, working out the movement of each actor. However, this tends to flatten out the overall design of the scene. This is because the director does not see an overview of the scene until he has spent a lot of time working out the details. By the time the director gets a sense of movement and pacing, he is already fairly far along. This approach tends to place camera decisions fairly late in the process.

An alternative to the character-by-character approach is to divide the action in the set into zones. Each zone can contain a submaster shot to establish the new space and subsequent coverage within the zone. The reason this makes sense is that most multi-character scenes are arranged around groupings of the characters, even if the groups change within the scene. The question is not "if" the actors are to be grouped, but "where" they will be grouped and in what arrangement.

The director can decide what part of the set will be used for each grouping and from what angle the action can be viewed. Now, when he rehearses the actors, they will be asked to move into the area or zone that the director would like to use for any given moment in the scene. Naturally, this will include the actors' suggestions and motivation, but the overall plan for the scene will be put on the table very early in the rehearsal. This is important because while individual actor's suggestions and movement are easy to comprehend, the pacing and overall spatial effect of the scene is illusive.

Organizing the scene space into zones can impose order on chaotic movement like a party sequence or busy street scene. It also tends to categorize movement into a plan that fits the requirements of shooting that the cinematographer and the assistant director will understand. Working this way, however, is just a starting point to organize dozens of shot possibilities quickly.

There may be two or three zones where several actors gather in a scene for a prolonged dialogue. Zones can be connected by camera movement, like dollying or panning, and these moves usually follow one of the characters. Or, two zones can be connected by reverse shots so that the foreground character in one zone becomes the background character in an adjacent shot.

Style, rhythm and performance should not be overshadowed by a structural plan, but when casts are large, a blueprint will help a director control the potentially large number of coverage options.

ZONES

The staging plan shown below in Figure 1 shows an aerial view of the set used in Staging 12. The shaded areas represent the zones in which the actors form into groups throughout the scene. While the actual boundaries of the zones are not precise and there are instances when an actor stands between zones, the majority of shots frame action taking place within the shaded areas.

Notice that all the shaded areas are shot from front or side angles so that only about two-thirds of the background has to be shot. As you can see, this is a three-wall set because there are no camera angles that include this space in the shot. Any of the shot, reverse-shot editing

Figure 1

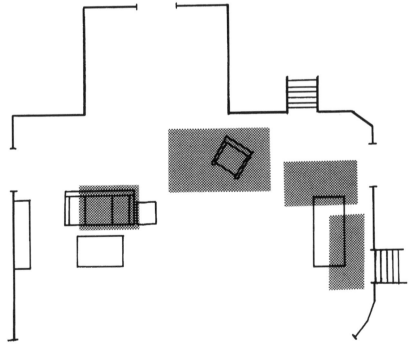

The grey blocks show the main staging areas or zones used in Staging 12.

patterns are arranged across the set (laterally left and right in the diagram) to minimize the scene space and to keep the backgrounds of shots contiguous.

Figure 2 below shows the camera positions used in Staging 12. When you consider that each of the camera setups indicates a shot that required rehearsal and some tweaking of the lighting, you can begin to appreciate the time necessary to shoot the scene. It should also be remembered that none of the camera positions used for coverage are included in the diagram. These additions could easily double or triple the number of setups.

Figure 2

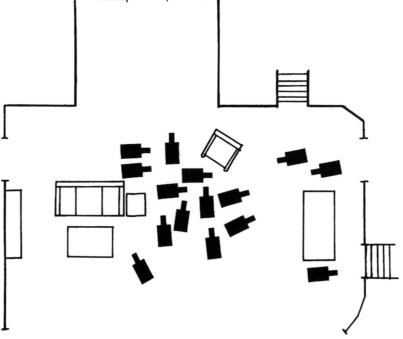

Each camera symbol indicates a camera setup used in Staging 12.

STAGING 12

In this next staging example, we will be working with six characters in a fairly busy dialogue sequence. This is a scene in which characters come and go, frequently forming a group for a short time and then repositioning themselves in a new group. This is a pretty taxing plan for a director, not the type of staging one would see on television, because it would simply take too much time to stage.

Staging 12 uses several camera moves to direct the viewer's attention, but unlike most of the stagings we have seen so far, there are no long masters to carry the scene. Instead, Staging 12 relies on cutting to connect drastic changes in view and moves to new zones in the scene space. The role of camera movement is to emphasize subjects or to isolate subjects within a space already established.

We can begin by acquainting ourselves with the floor plan of the scene space in which several zones have been identified. In general, Staging 12 utilizes considerable cutting and reverse angles. Front and side angles are used a great deal, juxtaposing right angle and 45-degree angle framings frequently. For the most part frontality is not favored.

1

Our scene opens with a couple, Jack and Grace, seated on a couch...

JACK: Will you be coming back?

GRACE: Not right away.

1a

...Jack stands and walks around to face the back of the room. The camera pans and dollies with him...

D1

Note: Read through the story-board a few times before spending much time on the diagrams, then go back and look at the camera placement. With a complex storyboard it takes a few read-throughs to make sense of the shot-flow.

This framing and the upcoming camera move would be easier to accomplish in a studio setting.

D1a

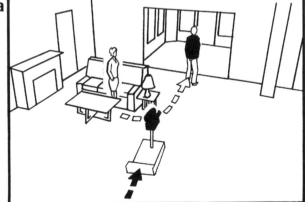

In this camera move, the operator would let Jack stand and move around the end table before beginning the move forward.

1b

...Grace comes around behind Jack during the camera move...

2

Cut to: A new angle of the door as a girl, Jane, enters. Grace is framed in the foreground.

D1b

An alternative camera move would wait for Jack to move into the background and begin moving forward as Grace steps into the frame.

D2

On a right-angle cut like this, Grace's placement in the frame could easily be cheated to line up the most desirable shot.

2a

The camera pans right with Jane as she goes to greet Jack. We cut shortly after the pan begins.

3

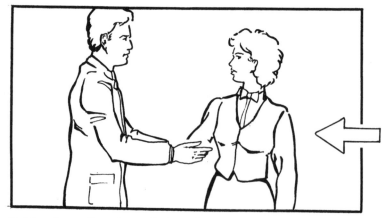

Cut to: A medium two-shot as Jane enters the shot and embraces Jack.

D2a

Coverage of this shot might include a locked-off shot and a second version in which the camera pans left with Jane.

D3

This shot is locked off, but an alternative version might include a small dolly move forward for emphasis.

4

Cut to: A wide three-shot. Jane begins to sit down. Grace exits the shot.

4a

...Jane sits down.

D4

This change in angle is motivated by Jane as she moves to sit in the chair. In fact, it is very nearly a cut on the action of her being seated.

D4a

The upcoming cut to a new angle is set up by some action such as Jane turning her head or turning to the new character's entrance. This shot might last only five seconds, as a bridge to the new angle in frame 5, as she begins to sit.

5

Cut to: A reverse angle (45 degrees). Jane completes the action of sitting. Walter enters in the background and comes forward.

5a

Walter greets Jack and Jane.

WALTER: I heard you guys were here.

D5

The new character, Walter, enters as Jane sits.

D5a

When Walter reaches Jack, we cut to the new angle. This shot might be only five to six seconds.

6

Cut to: A medium two-shot of Jack and Walter. They finish exchanging greetings...

6a

...Melissa enters in the background and comes up to Jack...

D6

Jack speaks for only a few seconds before Melissa enters.

D6a

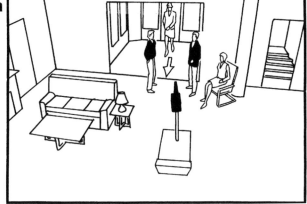

Notice that all the shots introducing the characters are brief shots from side angles. But as the group gathers, we move back to the front.

6b

...The camera dollies into a tighter, medium two-shot of Jack and Melissa.

7

Cut to: A wider shot of all four characters in the scene.

JACK: I don't believe all you guys are in town at once.
SFX. Door bell.

D6b

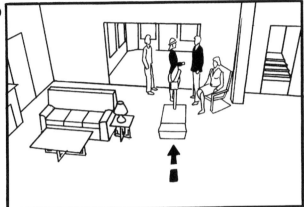

The camera moves forward about three feet to go from a wide, medium two-shot to a tight, medium two-shot. When the camera stops moving, we cut to the next shot. Shot 6-6b is seven seconds.

D7

This angular group shot is short because the doorbell rings right after the shot begins.

7a

...Walter crosses in back of the group to answer the door...

7b

...the camera pans with Walter and dollies forward to the top of the staircase...

D7a

We pan all the way over to the far right side of the set. Pan moves of this type are not typical of modern cutting patterns.

D7b

Once we make the pan move, we begin to dolly forward with Walter as he goes to the staircase.

7c

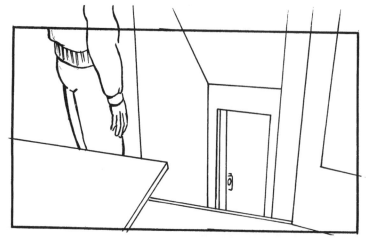

... the camera continues forward towards the stairs, tilting down to frame the door at the bottom of the stairs.

8

Cut to: A shot of the bottom of the stairs as Roy enters.

D7c

The camera moves forward over Walter's hip as the door opens. We cut to the new shot.

D8

This two-and-a-half second shot introduces the new character.

Note: Actors not involved in a shot may be excluded from diagrams. Also, figures are shaded black when they are within the camera frame but are shown as outlines when they are outside the frame.

9

Cut to: Walter at the top of the stairs. This is a repeat of the camera position in panel 7b. Walter exits the frame on the left.

10

Cut to: The group shot seen in frame 7. Walter enters the shot...

WALTER: It's Roy.

JACK: Don't tell him I'm here. I want to surprise him.

D9

This is a repeat of the framing in panel 7b. Now we pan with Walter, moving back to the group. This time, however, we let Walter exit the frame and let him reenter the frame in a new shot.

D10

This is a repeat of the shot (panel 7) from which we left the group. This is sometimes called a reestablishing shot. Walter immediately enters the frame.

10a

...Jack and Grace quickly leave the room.

11

Cut to: A new shot, framing Walter and Jane. Jane gets up from her seat as Jack and Grace are seen in the background, leaving the room...

D
10a

Walter tells everyone that Roy has arrived and Jack and Grace immediately leave. We cut as Jane gets out of the chair. So far, all our shots have been under nine seconds and several of the introductory shots have been less than five seconds.

D11

Jane completes the action of standing and Grace and Jack exit through a doorway. Notice that all the cuts bridge action. Meanwhile, Melissa has crossed right exiting the frame, but remains in the room.

11a

Walter steps into a two-shot with Jane.

JANE: Roy's going to wonder why we're here.

Walter: We'll tell him we came by to drop off Jack's car, and you came over to give me a ride.

11b

...Walter exits the shot.

D
11a

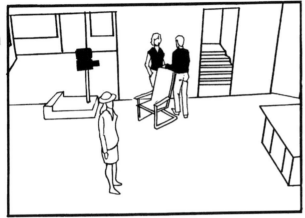

When a subject steps into a two-shot of this type, there is the option of moving the camera into a tighter shot, as seen earlier in panels 6a-6b. The extra move can be added as an alternate version of the shot.

D
11b

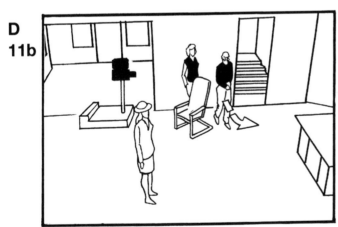

As the subject leaves the frame, the director has the option of panning to Jane to emphasize her or to move in on her reaction. But since we are going to stay with Walter, it makes sense to leave Jane in a locked-off frame.

12

Cut to: A new shot of the doorway as Roy comes into the room. Walter comes into the shot to greet Roy. Melissa is framed in the foreground.

13

Cut to: A medium reaction shot of Melissa looking on.

Notice that we are connecting two areas of the set that were previously connected by a pan. Since the pan established the spatial relationship between the spaces earlier, we can now use a cut which is a faster transition.

This is another situation where the placement of the figure can be cheated for compositional reasons. However, once the actors' "cheat position" is established for a given camera angle, positioning must remain consistent.

14

Return to the same framing as panel 12.
Roy walks forward to Jane. The camera dollies in a semi-circle to get a profile angle on the scene.

14a

Roy greets Jane...

ROY: Jane, this is great. I thought I'd missed you.

JANE: Look who else is here.

Roy turns to see Melissa. He comes forward...

D14

Roy approaches Jane. We saw her previously, standing on the far side of the chair. However, it is common practice to reposition an actor in the scene space while we cut away to another shot. In this case, the audience will accept that Jane has crossed ten feet of the set to greet Roy.

D 14a

Melissa (in the hat) might move forward a step and pivot to Roy as he approaches. This could also have been done during the camera move in panel 14.

14b

... Roy moves past Jane to greet Melissa. The camera move ends in a three-shot of Jane, Roy and Melissa.

15

Cut to: An OTS shot of Melissa.

D
14b

While this is pictured as an OTS shot, it would also be possible to move the camera forward to frame Roy in a closeup.

D15

This interesting setup places Roy between Walter and Melissa. This forces cutting between OTS shots as Roy shuttles between Walter and Melissa. It is a good strategy for isolating three subjects in a dialogue sequence.

ROY: This is great. But why didn't anyone call me?

MELISSA: Ask Walt, I'm just along for the ride.

15a

...Roy turns back to Walt to get an answer. The camera dollies back a couple of feet...

15b

The pull-back move ends when Roy is framed OTS of Walter.

ROY: What gives here?

WALTER: Melissa's goofing on you, this is all her idea.

**D
15a**

After Roy pivots and steps forward to Walter, the camera backs up with Roy moving into an OTS shot of Walter.

**D
15b**

The camera ends up in an OTS. This setup requires that the two outside subjects, in this case Melissa and Walter, have to be separated by at least five feet.

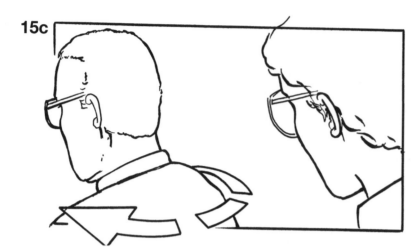

15c

After a moment Roy turns again.

16

Cut on Roy's turn to: A reverse OTS shot Roy turns and takes a step towards Melissa.

D
15c

Roy pivots a second time to turn back to Melissa. As shown, the new shot begins as an OTS shot, but we could easily repeat the camera movement that starts on Roy and pulls back to the OTS shot.

D16

We end the sequence in the OTS shot.

TECHNICAL CONSIDERATIONS

This final staging is a good example of how modest camera movement can be added to a relatively static staging. Compared with the kitchen sequence in Staging 9, which used long camera moves to reverse the camera view, Staging 12 uses small moves forward and back in depth to isolate or emphasize the players. This makes the camera moves relatively simple to execute. At the same time, the entire staging plan relies on considerable cutting rather than long takes.

This means that there will be time to shoot different versions of many of the shots, including those that use camera movement.

Review the diagrams and notice that the camera stays within a relatively small area at the center of the room and tends to point outward from the center like the hub of a wheel. There are only a few reverse shots and most of those are medium shots. This makes the set easier to light since only about half of the room will ever be seen.

CONCLUSION

If this were a book on watercolor technique or blues guitar, you would be able to immediately put the ideas presented here into practice. Unfortunately, the high cost of making films means that most filmmakers spend more time raising money than practicing their craft. While this struggle is an accepted part of independent filmmaking, new imaging technologies like video and multimedia on the desktop computer may for the first time change the rules in the filmmaker's favor.

Hi 8 and S-VHS camcorders produce a very respectable image relative to broadcast quality formats and the price of tape stock is insignificant. If you think about it, many of the small scenes in *Taxi Driver, Diner* or *Moonstruck* could have been shot with a video camera with very limited production resources. It's surprising how few filmmakers make short experimental films or sketches for their larger projects by taking advantage of inexpensive camcorders and off-line editing systems.

Camcorders are really part of a larger revolution that is taking place on the desktop computer. Multimedia is the term coined for the conversion of audio, print graphics, film, video and photography into a digital language that allows unprecedented control over sounds and images. It is now possible to edit video projects on a relatively inexpensive computer and to process the image in ways that formerly required tens of thousands of dollars of equipment.

This technology is only a few years old and advancing with dizzying speed with large and small breakthroughs occurring every few months. In the very near future, an individual or film cooperative will be able to have a multi-track sound studio, full-featured editing system, animation system and special effects capability relatively inexpensively on a desktop computer. Since these developments will drastically alter the price structure at existing film and video service companies, the cost of production is bound to come down.

Which more or less leads to my belief that the best way to learn about filmmaking is to make films or videos as often as possible. Staging can best be explored when there is a camera and a cast, however modest the production. I sincerely hope that you will take advantage of some of the new technologies to get your film made and hope *Cinematic Motion* will be of value to you on any of your future projects.

GLOSSARY

SHOT ABBREVIATIONS

ECU	—	Extreme close-up
CU	—	Close-up
MCU	—	Medium close-up
MS	—	Medium shot
WS	—	Wide shot
LS	—	Long shot
ELS	—	Extreme long shot
BG (bg)	—	Background
FG (fg)	—	Foreground
OTS	—	Over the shoulder
POV	—	Point of view

SHOT TERMS

CONTINUITY STYLE   The photographic and editorial style that creates the illusion of a spatial/temporal continuum so that a sequence of shots appears to present events as they happened. The continuity style is the predominant method in narrative film, sometimes called the Hollywood classical style or in France, decoupage classique.

COVERAGE   The alternate camera angles and setups obtained on set, beyond the basic requirements of the script or shot list, give the director the maximum flexibility to shape a scene during the editing process. As organized in the studio system, coverage follows a general shooting plan that includes an establishing master shot, group shots, and individual medium and closeup shots of each actor. Standard practice includes shooting the entire dialogue of all the actors, even those actors who are not expected to be on-screen for many of their lines.

CHEATING   The practice of rearranging the position of actors and props from shot to shot to obtain desired compositions without alerting the viewer that any change has occurred. Typical cheats include having an actor stand on a riser to appear taller in a medium shot or repositioning objects on a table, such as a pitcher or vase, to create framing devices.

REVEAL   A camera move that allows the viewer to see more information within the shot and is usually a dramatic effect to emphasize a story point.

SETUP   The camera viewpoint for any shot, taking into consideration the space to be included within the frame, the angle of view, the distance to the subject, the narrative stance, or point-of-view of the shot, and the focal length of the lens. In storytelling film, the setup also includes the positioning of the actors.

SINGLE, ONE-SHOT   A shot in which one subject fills the frame. A single can be any size: full-shot, medium or closeup.

TWO-SHOT, DOUBLE   A shot in which two subjects fill the frame, usually a medium shot.

THREE-SHOT   A shot framing three subjects in the frame.

MASTER, MASTER SHOT   A shot that is wide enough to cover all the important action in a scene. As a matter of procedure, the master is usually the first setup determined by a director and serves as the full record of a scene. Additional, closer shots of the action or partial action in the scene are then recorded, usually from new angles that relate spatially to the original master.

SEQUENCE SHOT, **LONG TAKE**   A shot designed to include several story points in a single, continuous take, rather than covering the same information in individual shots in an edited sequence.

CAMERA MOVES

CRAWL, **CREEP**   A very slow movement of the camera, often used to build tension.

COUNTER MOVE   The circular path of the camera, contrasted against the opposing movement of a subject.

CRANE UP, **CRANE DOWN**   The vertical movement of the camera on a crane.

BOOM UP, **BOOM DOWN**   The vertical movement of the camera on a boom. Since craning and booming essentially produce the same path, the terms are frequently used interchangeably.

DOLLYING, **TRACKING**, **TRUCKING**   Any camera movement on a dolly.

LATERAL MOVE   Any horizontal movement of the camera or a subject across the frame.

PAN   The rotational movement of the camera around a fixed point as on a tripod.

TRANSFER, **HAND-OFF**   A basic staging and compositional effect, in which a moving subject carries the viewer's attention from one place to another in the frame. For instance, at the opening of a scene, the camera follows a waiter walking through a restaurant. The waiter passes a couple at a table and the camera pans to the couple, making them the new subject of the shot. This technique can be used more than once in a shot to direct the viewer from story point to story point.

PUSH-IN The movement of the camera forward on a dolly, or the magnification of the image with a zoom lens.

PULL-BACK The movement of the camera away from a subject.

RACK FOCUS, **SHIFT FOCUS** Transferring the viewer's attention from one subject to another in a shot, by bringing one subject into focus while the other becomes blurred.

FOCUS PULL Changing the focus of the camera during a shot to keep specific subjects sharp as they move within the frame or while the camera moves.

F/STOP PULL Changing the size of the lens aperture to compensate for changes in the intensity of light during a shot; for example, when a camera travels from bright daylight into a dark cave.

RETRACKING In a dolly shot, the movement of the camera to a subject and then backwards over the same ground.

TILT UP, **TILT DOWN** Vertical panning.

WIDEN OUT The enlargement of the field-of-view by shortening the focal length of a zoom lens.

ZOOM The change of the field-of-view using a zoom lens.

SPATIAL TERMS

CROSSING THE LINE   Usually a cautionary term warning a director that he is selecting a camera view that is on the opposite side of the line of action than has been established while staging a scene. The term is cautionary because of the potential reversal of screen direction that may occur if shots from opposite sides of the line of action are edited together.

LINE OF ACTION, THE 180° RULE   An imaginary line, usually established along the sight lines between actors, that divides the total scene space in half. When the rule is observed, only camera setups on one side of the line will be used to cover the action in a scene. The purpose of this rule is to avoid a confusing reversal of screen direction that may result if shots from both sides of the line are cut together into a sequence.

DEEPER   (in the frame) Farther from the camera.

DOWNSTAGE   On the stage, the area closest to the audience.

UPSTAGE   On the stage, the area farthest from the audience.

ZONAL STAGING   Placement of the actors by designating areas in the set where action will take place.

X, Y, AND Z AXES   The three coordinate axes of motion in three-dimensional space. X(width), Y(height), Z(depth).

FRONTALITY   The convention in Western art that implies a favored view for the audience so that figures in a painting or a movie tend to face towards the viewer. The goal in classical storytelling is to give the illusion of "natural" figure placement while using frontality to reveal and emphasize story elements.

EDITING TERMS

ACTION CUT, **CUT ON ACTION**   The practice of making edit points during the movement of a subject, usually midway through the action, to hide the transition to a new angle of view. This technique, perfected in the German cinema during the 1920's, is one of the most basic editing principles in storytelling movies.

SHOT, **REVERSE SHOT PATTERN**   An editing pattern in which the camera view is alternated in opposing angles.

REVERSES   One-half a shot, reverse shot pattern. Movies are usually shot out of continuity and for technical reasons all the shots pointed towards a given direction are shot at the same time. Similarly, all the reverses would be shot at the same time.

ON-AXES CUT   The axes referred to are the optical axes of the camera. An on-axis cut moves the camera closer or farther away from the subject, while preserving the angle-of-view. (Also called an analytical cut.)

WIPE THE FRAME   The use of a moving foreground element that momentarily passes in front of the lens, obscuring the view of the subject of the shot. This serves the same purpose as the action cut and helps smooth the transition to a new shot in the scene.

MISCELLANEOUS

PRE-LIGHT   A period of time scheduled the day before the actual shoot day for rigging lights or special propping. Pre-lighting is often done over several hours the night before the shoot, giving the director more time to work on staging and performance the day of the shoot.

WILD WALLS   In a studio, any walls ceilings or other major architectural elements that can be detached from the set and moved to make room for lights, camera cranes, dollies or special effects rigging.

SHAKING THE MONEY TREE

How to Get Grants and Donations for Film & Video
by Morrie Warshawski

Dazed and confused by the frustrating world of grants and donations? This book demystifies the entire maze of grant world hustling and provides easy-to-follow guidelines. **WARSHAWSKI** is the nation's leading fund-raising consultant for media artists. Over the past two decades, he has assisted dozens of independent producers, created over 400 written proposals, participated on numerous grant panels, and advised countless institutional clients.

"Most how-to books are instantly disposable. Not this one. Put it on your shelf, under your pillow, give it to your trustees, and always have your copy handy. You'll be using it a lot." Brian O'Doherty, Director, Media Arts Program, Natiional Endowment for the Arts.

$24.95, 188 pages, ISBN 0-941188-18-3

FILM DIRECTING–SHOT BY SHOT:
Visualizing From Concept to Screen

by Steven D. Katz

About 380 pages, 7" x 10" paper
Approx. 400 illus. and photos
ISBN 0-941188-10-8, $24.95

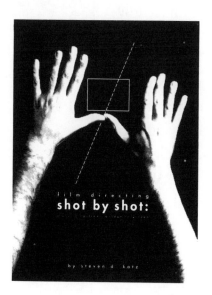

FILM DIRECTING SHOT BY SHOT is a complete catalogue of visual techniques and their stylistic implications for both film and video directors — "a text book" which enables working filmmakers (as well as screenwriters and producers) to expand their stylistic knowledge.

Extensively illustrated and well-written, it should find an enthusiastic audience among both seasoned and novice filmmakers.

Includes illustrations, photos and storyboards from:

- Alfred Hitchcock's *THE BIRDS* and *TORN CURTAIN*
- Steven Spielberg's *EMPIRE OF THE SUN*
- Orson Welles' *CITIZEN KANE*
- N.C. Wyeth and Howard Pyle artwork
- David Byrne's illustrations from *TRUE STORIES*

Contents include: Camera Techniques, Storyboard Style, Screen Ballistics, Framing and Compositional Techniques, Graphic Properties, Lenses, Moving Cameras, Style, How Directors Interpret Script Scenes, Blocking, Editing and Transitions, Image Organization, Symbolic Meaning, and Modern Techniques.

THE WRITER'S JOURNEY
Mythic Structure for Storytellers & Screenwriters
by Christopher Vogler
1992, approx. 200 pages
ISBN 0-941188-13-2, 6 x 8, $22.95
Available November 1992

Learn how the top Hollywood studios and screenwriters mine mythological treasures for story ideas. This practical writer's guide reveals the secret patterns of mythology including a powerful set of myth-inspired tools for structure and character that divulge the universal mythic structure behind all narrative writing.

Step-by-step guidelines show you how to structure your plot and create realistic characters. Innovative exercises help you troubleshoot and improve your own work. These ideas have been tested and refined by professional screenwriters, playwrights and novelists and will empower your command of storytelling through the ancient wisdom of myth. One of Hollywood's most powerful studio heads made the rough draft of this book *"required reading"* for the entire executive staff.

As a story analyst, **Chris Vogler** has evaluated over 6000 screenplays for major motion picture studios including Walt Disney, Warner Bros., 20th Century Fox, United Artists, Orion Pictures, The Ladd Company, Touchstone Pictures and Hollywood Pictures. He has also specialized in fairy tale and folklore consulting for Walt Disney Feature Animation.

Mr. Vogler is deeply indebted to the work of scholar Joseph Campbell and has enjoyed applying Campbell's ideas on mythology to screenwriting solutions. Mr. Vogler teaches classes in story analysis, motion picture development, and mythic structure in film at UCLA Extension Writers Program.

MICHAEL WIESE PRODUCTIONS offers a CONSULTING SERVICE to producers, directors, writers, media creators, distributors, suppliers, publishers and others to provide expert advice and strategies for film and home video. Clients include NATIONAL GEOGRAPHIC, THE SMITHSONIAN INSTITUTION, THE AMERICAN FILM INSTITUTE, MYSTIC FIRE VIDEO, PBS HOME VIDEO, WNE, KCET, THE APOLLO THEATER and many others. For more information call (818) 379-8799.

FILM & VIDEO FINANCING

By Michael Wiese
1991, Approx. 300 pages, 6 x 8 paper
ISBN 0-941188-11-6, $22.95

The most important—and most elusive—element in any producer's life is the ability to raise production monies.

Financing Film & Video offers the independent producer a plethora of approaches to the complex and arduous task of financing the low-budget features and home video programs.

Contents include information on current attitudes and approaches to finding investment through limited partnerships, equity investments, banking issues, split-rights deals, debt equity deals, blocked funds, foreign pre-sales, and much more.

Rounding out the volume are insider's tips from independent producers and money raisers for such films as *sex, lies and videotape, Dirty Dancing, Blue Steel, Trip to Bountiful,* and *Kiss of the Spider Woman*.

This is a book that should be on the desk of practicing film and video producers as well as anyone contemplating a venture into this field.

SUCCESSFUL FINANCING & DISTRIBUTION

THE INDEPENDENT FILM & VIDEOMAKERS GUIDE

By Michael Wiese
Revised Edition 1990, 392 pages, 45 illustrations.
ISBN 0-941188-03-5, $18.95

A classic best-seller and independent producer's best friend. Advice on limited partnerships, writing a prospectus, market research, negotiating, film markets, lists of pay TV and home video buyers.

- Financing
- Partnership Agreements
- Income Projections
- Investor Presentations
- Finding Distributors
- Promotion

"The book is full of practical tips on how to get a film or video project financed, produced, and distributed without sacrificing artistic integrity." **CO-EVOLUTION QUARTERLY**

FILM & VIDEO BUDGETS

By Michael Wiese
Revised 1990, 512 pages, 18 budgets
ISBN 0-941188-02-7, $18.95

This is a basic "how-to" budget guide for many types of films. Clearly written, informal in style, and generously illustrated with detailed budgets. Readers can look up sample budgets similar to their own and find a wealth of information on costs and savings. Includes:

- Money-Saving Tips
- Computer Budgets
- Line Items
- Accounting Procedures
- Negotiations
- Union/Guild Contacts

"...must reading. This is a common-sense book written with a touch of ironic humor. If you want to make your life easier in the financial arena of film/video making—buy the book.

Enjoyable reading for those who like profits." **INFO. FILM PRODUCERS ASSOC.**

ORDER FORM

To order these products please call 1-800-379-8808 or fax (818) 986-3408 or mail this order form to:

MICHAEL WIESE PRODUCTIONS
11288 Ventura Blvd., Suite 821
Studio City, CA 91604
1-800-379-8808

BOOKS:

_____
_____
_____
_____

Subtotal $_____
Shipping $_____
8.25% Sales Tax (Ca Only) $_____

TOTAL ENCLOSED_____

Please make check or money order payable to
Michael Wiese Productions

(Check one) ___ Master Card ___Visa _____Amex

Company PO#_____

Credit Card Number_____
Expiration Date_____
Cardholder's Name_____
Cardholder's Signature_____

SHIP TO:

CREDIT CARD ORDERS

CALL 1-800-379-8808

OR **FAX 818 986-3408**

OR E-MAIL
WIESE@EARTHLINK.NET

SHIPPING

1ST CLASS MAIL
One Book - $5.00
Two Books - $7.00
For each additional book, add $1.00.

AIRBORNE EXPRESS
2nd Day Delivery
Add an additional $11.00 per order.

OVERSEAS (PREPAID)
Surface - $7.00 ea. book
Airmail - $15.00 ea. book

Name_____
Address_____
City_____State_____Zip_____
Country_____Telephone_____
CALL 1-800-379-8808 for a Free Book & Software Catalog

VISIT OUR HOME PAGE http://www.earthlink.net/~mwp

Please allow 2-3 weeks for delivery.
All prices subject to change without notice.